WHO CARES?
Cultivating the Fine Art of Loving One Another

WHO CARES?

Cultivating the Fine Art of Loving One Another

GAYLE G. ROPER

Harold Shaw Publishers
Wheaton, Illinois

All Scripture quotations are taken from the *Holy Bible, New International Version*. Copyright © 1973, 1978, 1984, International Bible Society. Used by permission of Zondervan Publishing House. All rights reserved.

Coyright © 1992, Gayle G. Roper

All rights reserved. No part of this book may be reproduced or transmitted in any form or by any means, electronic or mechanical, including photocopying, recording, or any information storage and retrieval system without written permission from Harold Shaw Publishers, Box 567, Wheaton, Illinois 60189.

ISBN 0-87788-948-1

Cover design by Ron Kadrmas

Library of Congress Cataloging-in-Publication Data

Roper, Gayle G.
   Who cares? : cultivating the fine art of loving one another / Gayle G. Roper.
     p.   cm.
   Includes bibliographical references.
   ISBN 0-87788-948-1
   1. Caring—Religious aspects—Christianity.   I. Title.
BV4647.S9R66 1992
241'.4—dc20   91-44745
                                                                     CIP

99 98 97 96 95 94 93 92

10 9 8 7 6 5 4 3 2 1

for Mom Roper,
with admiration for your enthusiasm,
energy, and commitment to the things of God

with special thanks
to the Wednesday morning Bible study
who let me practice this material on them
and
to Bebe, Ginny, Jean, Nancy, and Vicki
who prayed

Contents

1 caring = meeting a genuine need___*1*

2 caring = being there___*9*

3 caring = loving one another___*19*

4 caring = forgiving one another___*29*

5 caring = accepting one another___*41*

6 caring = admonishing one another___*51*

7 caring = serving one another___*59*

8 caring = submitting to one another___*71*

9 caring = encouraging one another___*81*

10 caring = taking a chance___*93*

notes___*99*

1

caring = meeting a genuine need

I TURNED FIFTY AWHILE AGO. NO GREAT TRAUMA. I KNOW I'M really thirty inside.

For the length of our marriage, Chuck and I have viewed birthdays differently. He forgets them; I celebrate them. This difference of vision made the first years of our marriage stressful once every twelve months (twice if you want to count anniversaries, which he also forgot).

Finally I realized a truth about Chuck: the only occasion he will unfailingly remember is Christmas, and the only reason he remembers that one is because all of America helps him remember.

Hard on the heels of this realization came another: there was no malice in his forgetting. He simply had other things on his mind. He is, after all, an engineer.

I pondered my new understanding of my husband and came to what seemed—and seems—an eminently practical solution to my quandary. I would tell him in advance of all approaching events.

Near the end of September I say, "Gosh, my birthday's only three weeks away. I can't believe another year's passed!"

Chuck looks startled. "Your birthday's coming?"

I nod. "Amazing isn't it? October 15, just like last year."

"Mm," he mumbles. "October 15."

About October 8, I say, "Just think, my birthday's only a week from today."

"A week, you say?" Chuck looks surprised. This is news.

I nod. "A week." Reinforcement.

"What do you want for a present?" he asks, almost interested. "How about a new mixer? Or a toaster?"

"No," I say. "No appliances. Clothes. Dinner out. Money. But no appliances."

He looks at me strangely. After all, he loves tools and appliances, can live happily without eating out, and thinks I have enough clothes already.

That's what makes what he did for my fiftieth birthday so special. He did what I would enjoy, not what he would enjoy.

He hosted a surprise party for me, an after-church brunch at a restaurant that I love. He invited my friends as opposed to just ours, including several single women and writers I appreciate. He even let everyone bring presents because I love presents. And I didn't get one appliance.

It means much to me that Chuck cared enough to have a party for me. It meant more that he tailored the occasion to me. He even ordered a chocolate cake because I like it so much—and he can't eat chocolate.

Chuck fulfilled the prime requisite for caring: meeting the other person's needs, making the other person happy, doing what the other person wants. Caring is, above all, other-oriented.

caring = meeting a genuine need

It's nice when caring can be done at such a pleasant and leisurely pace. Frequently, though, caring is not convenient.

It was Thanksgiving Eve a few years ago. The phone rang as I was preparing dinner. After we ate, we were planning to go to the annual Thanksgiving service, a special time when people in our church family share what God has done for them over the last year. It's one of the year's highlights.

Jeff, then seventeen, took the call. I could tell by the quality of his voice that it was his girlfriend Cindy, but I was surprised at the brevity of the conversation. They were at the whispering-nothing-by-the-hour stage.

"Cindy's mom just fell in the driveway and broke her knee," Jeff said. "Cindy called to ask us to pray."

Bad news. "What caused Lois to fall?"

"She slipped. That's all I know." He was quiet for a minute. "Cindy's dad wasn't home, and they don't know how to reach him. He's running a bunch of errands."

It took a moment or two for the significance of the last statement to reach me. "You mean Cindy's alone with Lois?"

He nodded. "She sounded scared."

I'll bet. "You want to go to the hospital to be with her?"

"Yes." He sounded somewhat scared, too.

I looked at him, and it was clear this was not a time just to give him the car keys. We found Cindy and Lois at the second hospital we tried and spent the next couple of hours with them while Lois waited for treatment and her husband, and Cindy's pulse rate returned to normal. Chuck found our note when he got home and joined us.

Instead of our cozy dinner and the Thanksgiving service, we had the Emergency Room and a quick bite at MacDonald's. That's caring. Whatever's needed. Whenever it's needed.

Besides the inconvenience of caring, there may be a tremendous risk taken when we care. In reaching out to help, we make ourselves vulnerable and leave ourselves exposed. What if we're not appreciated? What if the one we're trying to help doesn't receive our help properly? What if we're embarrassed? Misunderstood?

When Jill and Harold learned that the unmarried daughter of Christian friends was pregnant, they invited their friends over for dinner. During the evening, the friends brought up their daughter's situation.

"They want to get married, but we don't know if that's the best solution."

"We want to tell you that Maddie's pregnancy need not be the end of her future," Harold said. "We want to encourage you by telling you about us."

He paused and smiled at Jill, then continued, "Twenty years ago, that was our situation. Jill was pregnant when we got married. We didn't live in this area then, so we know you're not aware of our story. We just want you to know that situations like this one can work, and that God is a great God."

When Maddie's parents reflect on their daughter's long-ago pregnancy, one of the brightest moments in that hard time was the night at Jill and Harold's when loving Christians cared enough to make themselves vulnerable. It would have been safer for Jill and Harold to protect their secret. Instead they chose to put their "testimony" in danger for the sake of need and the opportunity to offer genuine help.

Another characteristic of caring is the fact that it's an action word. Webster defines caring not only as *feeling* concern but also as *providing* for that concern. In a biblical sense *caring is thoughtfully doing something for another with a need and doing it in the name of Christ, expecting and anticipating nothing in return*. Caring requires that we develop a sensitivity to others and that we become committed "not to reducing our fears, but

caring = meeting a genuine need

to doing whatever we can to reduce the fears in others, or to fulfill their needs."[1]

This shift in vision from ourselves and our desires to others and their needs goes against the natural instinct to make certain we get what we deserve, what we want, what we lack.

> A man was going down from Jerusalem to Jericho, when he fell into the hands of robbers. They stripped him of his clothes, beat him and went away, leaving him half dead.
>
> A priest happened to be going down the same road, and when he saw the man, he passed by on the other side.
>
> So too, a Levite, when he came to the place and saw him, passed by on the other side.
>
> But a Samaritan, as he traveled, came where the man was; and when he saw him, he took pity on him. He went to him and bandaged his wounds, pouring on oil and wine. Then he put the man on his own donkey, took him to an inn and took care of him. The next day he took out two silver coins and gave them to the innkeeper. "Look after him," he said, "and when I return, I will reimburse you for any extra expense you may have." *Luke 10:30-35*

It is worth noting that the priest and the Levite did nothing to hurt the injured man. They may even have felt badly for him. They merely took the easiest and safest course of action.

The Samaritan, on the other hand,

- *took pity on the injured man.* His heart responded to the needs of another.
- *gave his time, supplies, and money.* He willingly accepted the cost and inconvenience to his schedule and pocketbook.

- *made himself vulnerable.* What if the robbers were still about? He could have been beaten and robbed, too. What if people misunderstood a Samaritan assisting a Hebrew? The two belonged to ethnic groups that were, after all, enemies.
- *took action.* Jesus himself commended the mercy-giving of the Good Samaritan to us as a model. "Go and do likewise," he said.

Of course the greatest example of one who gave of himself because of the needs of others is Jesus. He saw our great spiritual bankruptcy and chose to suffer pain and death to allay our poverty. Through the vast bounty of his care, he made it possible for us to leave the hovels of sin for the abundances of grace.

> But because of his great love for us, God, who is rich in mercy, made us alive with Christ even when we were dead in transgressions—it is by grace you have been saved. And God raised us up with Christ and seated us with him in the heavenly realms in Christ Jesus, in order that in the coming ages he might show the incomparable riches of his grace, expressed in his kindness to us in Christ Jesus." *Ephesians 2:4-7*

The goal of this book you are reading is twofold. The first is to study what the Word of God says about caring. The pattern chosen to fulfill this goal is an examination of the many New Testament verses that use the phrase *one another,* as in "encourage one another" or "bear with one another" or "forgive one another" or "love one another."

The second goal is actually to practice caring, to learn how the principles of the Bible work in real life, to *do.* Questions and recommendations at the end of each chapter are designed to help us "go and do likewise."

Summary

Genuine caring has four characteristics:

1. It is done to satisfy the receiver, not the giver.
2. It is frequently inconvenient.
3. It may make the giver vulnerable.
4. It requires action, not merely feeling.

Caring is defined as thoughtfully doing something for another with a need and doing it in the name of Christ, expecting and anticipating nothing in return.

The Good Samaritan is an excellent case study, and Jesus' injunction to "go and do likewise" requires our response in obedience.

Jesus himself cared for us to the point of giving up his life.

Questions, Questions . . .

1. Read 1 Thessalonians 3:12 and Galatians 6:10. According to these verses, for whom are we to care?
   all in need—

2. Do you think you are to care for every need you see? Why or why not? *No*

3. Why do you think some people's needs go unmet?

4. Read 1 Peter 5:7. What is the practical significance of this verse in light of the definition of caring?
   Remember to give your anxiety to God. Do in the name of Christ

5. How does biblical caring correspond with the American credo of self-reliance and independence?

6. What if you show care and no one ever returns the favor? Read Galatians 6:9. When is "the proper time"?

7. If you are reading this book as an individual (as opposed to a member of a Bible study), determine to do something that demonstrates care to someone. Look around you and reach out. Do something you normally would not do for someone several times over the next month. It need not be the same person every time.

8. If you are reading this book as part of a Bible study, at each meeting draw a participant's name. Do something caring for that person before the next meeting. Also do something caring for someone outside your Bible study circle.

2

caring = being there

SEVERAL YEARS AGO I WAS READING A BOOK BY ONE OF MY THEN-favorite authors. In the book, the writer kept referring to all the wonderful things friends had done for her. People bought her this and gave her that. They ran errands for her and cleaned her house. They told her how gifted she was and how interesting all her writings were. It seemed every time she turned around, something special was happening for her.

As I read about all this wonderfulness, I began to get distressed.

No one ever does any of these things for me, I pouted to myself. *How come she lives near all the neat people and I live near the rest? No one takes care of me, serves me, holds my hand, tells me I'm wonderful. It's not fair!*

Very gently the Holy Spirit brought some thoughts to my mind. *What,* he asked me, *have you done for someone lately? Who have you taken care of, served, held hands with, told she's wonderful?*

Be wary, he said, *of that huge beam in your eye, Gayle. You're the one who's not being fair.*

Talk about being brought up short.

So I began to think about the concept of caring and quickly realized one truth. We all want to be cared for, but few of us want to expend the energy to care for others.

I have no trouble understanding why we enjoy being cared for. We all want to be liked, appreciated, made to feel important. We all want presents and flowers and pats on the head. And when we hurt, we all want an arm around our shoulders and a listening ear who appears to care genuinely.

So why don't we automatically reach out? Why do we just let each other sit back and feel hurt or desperate or rejected as we live our insular lives?

We will look at seven possible reasons why we hesitate to help. All are, of course, rooted in the doctrine of Original Sin, that curse of Me First that separates us from God. Even after we have trusted Christ as our Savior, we are tainted by the compulsion to protect our own backs and seek our own good. From these very human tendencies come our hesitancies.

First, we are slow to help others because *we fear rejection.*

- *What if she doesn't like the meal I fix?*
- *What if he thinks my offer to repair his roof is butting into his private life?*
- *What if I say, "Here, these coupons are for you," and all she does is stare at me?*
- *What if I buy him this book and he thinks I'm criticizing him? After all, it is a tender topic.*
- *What if I say I'd like to pay her rent for her this month and she says, "No!"*

All these scenarios could well happen. We could be rejected when we offer help. People often get their hackles up when someone in any way suggests that they can't cope by themselves, even when they can't and they know it.

I've come to realize, though, that the issue isn't what the other person might or might not want me to do. It's what Christ would want me to do. If he has told us to care and has exemplified care, then we should live out this idea. If we are rejected when we offer to help, so what? Seriously. I mean it.

So what?

The psalmist wrote: "The LORD is with me; I will not be afraid. What can man do to me?" (Psalm 118:6).

What can people do to us? They can reject us as we seek to help in Jesus' name. But so what? The Lord is with us!

The second reason we may have difficulty caring for others may be that *we were never taught to recognize need.*

Many very nice people grew up in homes where there was minimal involvement in the lives of others. Life was more a matter of keeping the masks in place and respecting the masks of others than of seeing and meeting needs.

"I grew up in a family where being reserved was prized," said Meg. "Don't ask me what's wrong in my life, and I won't ask you what's wrong in yours. Even sending a card of encouragement was improper because that indicated you knew something about the other people's lives.

"It's only since I've become a Christian that I've learned that I should be interested in what's wrong with others, not to gloat or wring my hands over, but so I can help. I've had to watch Christian friends who knew how to help so that I could learn how. They're like Paul to me when he said, 'Follow my example, as I follow the example of Christ' " (1 Corinthians 11:1).

The third possible reason for not caring is *fear of embarrassing ourselves or the ones we help.*

Lissa's son was arrested on drug charges, and the story made the local papers. Needless to say, it was a moment of great sorrow for Lissa and the rest of her family.

"I received a note from only one person," Lissa told me. "Only one. All it said was, 'I'm so sorry. I'm praying for you and your family, especially your son.' What a balm to my spirit it was in a terribly hurtful time. No one else in our church or community even mentioned the situation. It was like our troubles didn't exist. I realize that most people were afraid of embarrassing either themselves or me, but I know I could have used the support."

Being too busy may be another reason for not caring. Many of us live such fast-paced lives. We have wonderful technology, a fantastic standard of living, and more options than any other people in history, but the price is often our relationships.

When we work full-time jobs, have families and homes to care for, are involved in kid activities, church activities, and community activities, when do we have time even to *see* someone's pain, let alone *respond* to it? Fatigue and pressure force people to the periphery of our lives. Survival, not serving, becomes our main goal.

Obviously such a lifestyle isn't healthy for any number of reasons, but one is that it causes us to be disobedient to the exhortations of Scripture to care for each other.

Some people don't take the time to care for others because, quite frankly, *they are too selfish or too angry to care about anyone.*

- *Why in the world should I do something for him? He's never done anything for me.*

- *Hey, she brought it on herself. Don't expect me to bail her out.*

Anger and/or selfishness make us petty and turn what was originally just a little chip on the shoulder into a great forest in which we hide lest we be taken advantage of (horrors, horrors!).

The sixth reason why some people don't reach out is a sad one. It afflicts people who have been carers in the past. They've poured hours and resources and prayer into numerous situations. However when they themselves had a critical need, no one noticed. No one came forward to help, and no one seemed to care. Great hurt was the result.

Now these former servants shutter their eyes because *they were so hurt that they will no longer respond.* Their emotions are raw, their hearts wounded. The unspoken pact, at least in their minds, was that if I care for you, you will care for me. And you didn't. The pact has been broken and the hurt is intense.

But the reality of servanthood is that there is no pact. There is no guarantee. There is no assurance of returned interest.

That's why part of the definition of caring is "expecting nothing in return."

That's why Paul had to write, "Let us not become weary in doing good, for at the proper time we will reap a harvest if we do not give up. Therefore, as we have opportunity, let us do good to all people, especially to those who belong to the family of believers" (Galatians 6:9-10).

There is a seventh reason why people don't care for each other, a reason that skews the line of responsibility a bit. Frequently people don't care because *they don't know there is a problem.*

It hurts and humbles to admit I have a great need in my life that I can't manage. I don't want to tell you I'm overwhelmed and need you to keep me from being swept away in the flood.

I don't want to admit my husband is being unfaithful, or my teen-aged child is hitting me, or I've just lost my job, or my health is so bad that I can no longer care for my family.

And it can also be just as difficult to admit the small needs. How do I say I weigh too much, or I'm in debt, or I can't get along with my mother-in-law, or my kids sass me all the time?

After all we live in a society that praises personal independence. My own two feet and by my own bootstraps and I'm a self-made person.

But what about God? What does he say?

> Cast all your anxiety (or care) on him because he cares for you. *1 Peter 5:7*
>
> So that there should be no division in the body, but that its parts should have equal concern (or care) for each other. *1 Corinthians 12:25*

God didn't design us to be stoic, independent individuals. He created us to be needy. He wants us to need him and he will respond to that need by caring for us with a well-planned, deep concern. He also wants us to need each other so that each in the body of believers will be distracted from himself and drawn in the direction of another's need.

Perhaps you can visualize God's plan by imagining two intersecting lines (Figure 1). One line is vertical, the other horizontal. The vertical line represents each person and his or her relationship with God. The horizontal line represents each person and his or her contact with others.

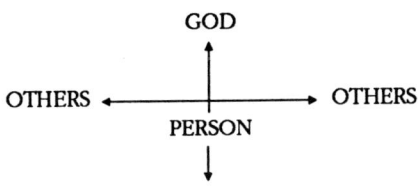

Figure 1

Imagine there are arrows on both ends of both lines. These arrows represent the give and take of the relationships. Thoughts, emotions, encouragement, and caring flow back and forth between those at either end of the lines.

A strong vertical line—or a vibrant association with God—begins with an understanding that we cannot have a relationship with God apart from faith in Jesus Christ. Our imperfection offends God's perfection. So Jesus died on Calvary, bearing our sin, that when we believe in him, we might be made the righteousness of God.

With belief we begin our tenuous acquaintance with God, and it can daily grow into an intimacy that dominates our lives.

From this strong vertical relationship come healthy horizontal ones. We become friends, not for what we might get out of each other, but because God wants us to love each other. There is an equity and a wholeness in our associations because of Christ.

Because I love God, I can love you.

Because God cares for me, I can care for you.

Because he accepts me regardless of my situation and problems, I can tell you where I hurt and accept your help.

Because he touches and strengthens my heart, I can reach out to you in your pain.

Because he strengthens me, I can pass along some of that strength to you.

In other words, God's plan is that he will meet your needs, sometimes by ministering himself to your heart and spirit and sometimes through those of us who are his. Any failure in this plan is not his.

Summary

There are several reasons we don't care for each other.

1. We fear rejection.
2. We were never taught to care.
3. We fear embarrassing ourselves or others.
4. We're too busy.
5. We're too selfish or angry.
6. We've been hurt.
7. No one has told us there is a need.

God's plan to care for us is based on a strong relationship with him so he can minister to our hearts and a strong relationship with others so we can help each other.

Questions, Questions . . .

1. What do you consider to be your greatest deterrent to caring?

2. List all the servant-type things you have done over the past week. Include little things like sending a get-well card or driving your daughter and her friends to the mall as well as big things like sitting with a dying friend or paying off someone's electric bill.

3. How many times did you help someone in spite of how you felt? Does this make you a hypocrite?

4. Who is the greatest model of a Christian care-giver you know? What characterizes his or her life?

5. How are you going to make room in your schedule to help others?

6. Ask five people for one or two of the most helpful or special things ever done for them. Note the variety of services. Note the manner in which your five people speak of their carers.

7. What do you enjoy doing for people? How can you do this for someone who is dealing with chronic illness? or someone in a financial bind? or someone with kid troubles?

3

caring = loving one another

♥

SEVERAL YEARS AGO, CHIP (NOW TWENTY-FOUR YEARS OLD) WAS having one of those nights little kids have. Every time I managed to fall asleep, he needed me. If it wasn't concern over the airplane that he dreamed was flying in his window, it was the fact that we were heartlessly allowing him to die of thirst right there in his own bed.

Finally I decided it was time to share the burden and shook Chuck.

"Chip needs you," I mumbled.

It always amazed me how my husband could sleep through the tragic, high-decibel cries of his children, but if the oil burner or the water pump burped unexpectedly, he was on his feet in an instant, alert and ready to do battle.

"Chip needs you," I mumbled again. I shook Chuck and got no response, so I placed my feet in the small of his back and began pushing ever so slowly toward his edge of the bed.

I don't know how to put the snorts and snuffles he made into words, but I'm sure you understand.

Finally, when he started to fall, he realized what was happening. He pulled himself erect, looked down at me, and said with all the venom of a rudely awakened person, "I don't know why you don't take care of him. He's your son."

He then stormed from the room, and I lay listening with great interest to see if he was about to inflict on the child a psychological wound from which he'd spend his whole life recovering.

But the twenty or thirty feet from bed to bed worked their magic, and Chuck reached Chip's side as his normal self.

"What can I do for you, honey?" I heard. "Tell Daddy what's the matter." Honey never flowed so smoothly and sweetly.

Why do parents all over the world tumble from their sleep every night to minister to countless kids? I assure you it's not because they relish the lack of sleep. I've yet to hear a mom say she felt the circles under her eyes enhanced her beauty.

No one faces whiny, weepy, or bright-eyed kids at 3 A.M. because they *feel* like it. A parent may be desperate, fatigued, angry, helpless, numb, but none is joyful. A child is cared for in the middle of the night for one overriding reason: the child has a need and the parent chooses to meet that need as well as can be done without proper sleep and with the resultant lack of judgment.

And this choice to minister is the core definition of biblical love. Biblical love is *my choice to act for your good.* It is my deliberate exercise of will to serve you.

When a parent rushes to a child's room in the middle of the night, of course there is emotion. This little being has a special place in the heart, and the care response is partially triggered by that affection, at least the first three times.

But affection need not be present in biblical love. It may be there. In fact, frequently it is there. But it doesn't need to be.

That's why it's possible to behave with love toward a person we don't even like.

> This is how we know what love is: Jesus Christ laid down his life for us. *1 John 3:16*

There is no more beautiful picture of what it means to love one another than the portrait Christ drew for us.

He didn't want to die. In fact, he sweat drops of blood as he yearned for a way out. But there wasn't one. Unless he died, mankind could never know God.

By a conscious choice of his will, God allowed his Son to die. By a resolute commitment of his will, Jesus allowed himself to be nailed to a cross.

The reason the Godhead endured such pain? Our need.

This undeserved love shown us was gracious beyond understanding, inconvenient beyond our wildest imaginations, and solely for our benefit. "Love, to be all it was meant to be, is nonnegotiably unconditional."[1] It must be openhanded.

If loving one another is so demanding and difficult, leading God himself to death, why do I want to do it? Why should I bother? Why should I subject myself to something so arduous?

> This is my command: Love each other. *John 15:17*

The reason for loving isn't very complex, is it? It's obedience. And the model for this love is equally clear.

> As I have loved you, so you must love one another.
> John 13:34

As Christ loved, so should we. Whew! But love is so practical, so sensible, so beneficial to everyone. It's the hub of the wheel of Christian living (Figure 2).

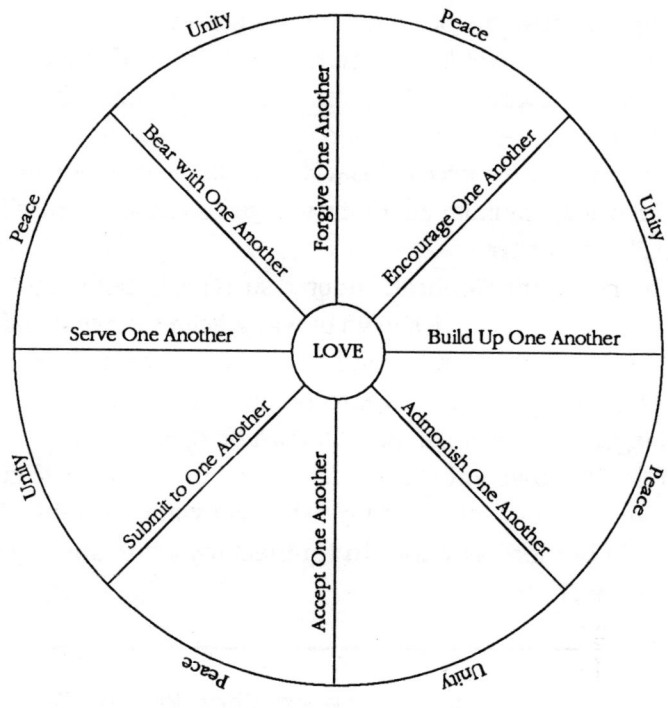

Figure 2

Once Chuck and I were ice skating with some friends on the Lehigh Canal in Bethlehem, Pennsylvania. We were young, recently married, and we had a black and white dog named Fluffy we took everywhere with us, including skating. Fluffy loved running on the ice and sliding, her ears flapping happily in the frosty air.

Someone, for some unknown reason, had hacked a hole in the middle of the frozen canal, and we were all careful to avoid it, even Fluffy. However, on one of her races along the ice, she got too close to the hole, couldn't stop on the slick surface, and went in.

Fortunately she didn't go under the ice itself but bobbed in the open water, scrabbling at the edges of the hole for escape. We were some distance away and raced toward her, already reaching out to help.

I have in my mind's eye a movie version of the experience. I see all the people skating happily on the canal, the sun shining. I see the happy dog, racing and sliding. I see Chuck and me and our friends, laughing and falling. I see a dark cloud appear, sending snow flurries. I see us shivering. I see the gaping hole. I see Fluffy sliding inexorably into the water. I see my horrified face, my reaching hands, my race to save her.

I no longer know how much of what I remember is accurate beyond Fluffy falling in the hole and my feeling of fear. I don't know if there were dark clouds and snow flurries. Obviously I couldn't see myself as I do in my mind's eye. I just know the fear, the reaching, and the dog pulling herself out onto the ice before we even got close to her. She shook herself off and smiled, ready for more fun.

But imagine with me what Chuck and I would have done had the dog been unable to get herself out. We would have reached out to her, stretched out as far as we could, eager to get her to safety.

That's the picture of how we are to love each other.

> Love one another deeply, from the heart. *1 Peter 1:22*

Deeply has the idea of stretched out or strained. From our heart we are to reach out to each other, pull each other out of the freezing water, dry each other off, and help each other get going again.

You have a problem? Here's my hand. Grab on. I'll pull you to safety.

When we love each other this way, two major things will happen.

1. We will be an example without parallel to the world.
2. We will experience spiritual health within the church.

Many people are understandably engrossed with the doctrine of the end times. When will Jesus come again? What is the Tribulation and how am I affected by it? What do all the strange descriptions in Revelation really mean? Who will be the Antichrist? What is the Mark of the Beast?

I have some other questions for you. What about Christians in the present time? What about loving one another? Where is the Mark of the Believer?

Love one another, Jesus told his disciples. Love each other as I love you.

> All men will know that you are my disciples if you love one another. *John 13:35*

The proof of who we are in Christ isn't how many folks have come to the Lord through us. It isn't how much we've contributed to the Lord's work. It isn't how sweetly we've sung his praises. It is, pure and simple, how we have loved each other.

A couple more questions for you:

- How many of you have been involved in some way in a church split?
  Love one another.
- How many of you know Christians who don't speak to each other?
  Love one another.
- How many of you know people in your congregation who actively and verbally dislike your pastor?
  Love one another.

I have a theory about Christian living. I think that if every Christian loved every other Christian as God would wish, there would be no unmet needs within the church.

The Lord would bring certain people in need to you and certain ones to me. When I'm in need, he would bring my plight to the mind of those who could care for me, and the same for you in your time of need. There would be so much stretching out and reaching out for the other guy's benefit that the world would shake its head in wonder, and the church would be as whole as possible in this world.

One catch to this theory—and there are several—is that it frequently is hard to figure out *how* to love each other. If biblical love isn't a feeling or a hug (though it may be both), how do I recognize it, let alone practice it?

Simple. Just love your neighbor as yourself.

What do you like people to do for you?

When you're sad, what makes you feel better?

When you're having kid troubles, what would ease your hurt and frustration (besides giving away the kid)?

When you are ill, what kindnesses are the biggest helps?

When someone you love has betrayed you, what would ease your pain?

Offer this same loving care to others. Do for them what you would hope someone would do for you. Choose their good at your inconvenience, at your penalty, at your expense.

For there is a cost in caring like this. Loving one another leaves us wide open:

- to be taken advantage of
- to be worn out
- to be misunderstood
- to be rejected
- to be Jesus to someone

What an honor.

Summary

Biblical love is my choice to act for your benefit. It is my deliberate exercise of will to serve you.

Jesus is the perfect example of One who showed love for the benefit of another.

We are to love out of obedience and as Christ loved—deeply.

When believers love like this, the world will see and know we are Christians, and the church will be healthy.

caring = loving one another

Questions, Questions . . .

1. Look up the following verses. How do they help you understand the various dimensions of the love God requires?
   - Matthew 22:37
   - John 15:12
   - Luke 6:27

2. What is the biblical relationship between love and like?

3. How do you love someone when you have a distinct difference of opinion that will not go away?

4. How do you love someone when he or she is involved in behavior that is flat out wrong? Is there a difference in response when this someone is your child as opposed to another adult?

5. Read 1 Peter 4:8. What very practical outcome of love do you find here?

4

caring = forgiving one another

♥

SEVERAL YEARS AGO WHEN I DID SOME SIT-UPS WITHOUT PROPERLY warming up, I pulled a muscle in my left upper back. The pull was so severe that for a while I couldn't even pick up a dress without pain.

In the process of treating this injury, x-rays were taken, and the doctors discovered I had a malformation in my spine right between my shoulder blades. I'd always been active, lifting and pulling with no discomfort, even carrying heavy trays as a waitress for five summers when I was a student, so this discovery was a great surprise.

Suddenly things changed dramatically, and they've never returned to "normal." The muscle pull is long gone, but its effect on the weak part of my spine has been permanent. As anyone with a back injury knows, such a problem never goes away; it just goes on and on.

I've had to learn I can't carry in the groceries anymore. I can't sit on deep sofas and chairs because, with my short legs, I lean into the back cushions right at my vulnerable spot. I can't sit on one hip with both legs to one side because of the tension this twisted position puts on my upper back. I can't work in the church nursery because I can't hold the heavier babies.

When my back acts up, which it does with frustrating frequency, I am in much discomfort. The muscles then tense and the pain worsens, traveling up my neck to my head, finally interfering with my ability to concentrate. Then I seek relief from my chiropractor. After a couple of adjustments, I'm fine until the next time I lift something I shouldn't, or I lean on my elbows when they're propped on my desk, or I sleep in a twisted position.

The distress of a back out of joint presents a good image of the distress of a Christian who doesn't forgive. There's a tension, a pressure bearing on an area of weakness, and the result is pain and the inability to function anywhere near the peak of potential.

One of the meanings of the verb "forgive" is *to send away or to release from a justly deserved penalty.*

Say someone owes me money. If I forgive that debt, I release my debtor from the payment of a legitimately incurred responsibility. I "send away" the debt.

When God forgives us, he sends away our deserved penalty and releases us from our debt. When Christ prayed, "Forgive us our debts as we also have forgiven . . ." (Matthew 6:12), he was saying that as God sends away our sins, so should we send away the sins of those who have hurt us. Though they have earned punishment, we choose to forgive.

Another meaning of forgive is *to show favor or to give freely,* and this meaning comes from the same root word as grace. It means that we are to forgive with the same free and gracious favor with which Christ forgives us.

God has never and will never yell, "Okay, I forgive you! But you'd better never do it again!" or, "Okay, I'll forgive, but I won't forget!" Rather he says, "I've chosen not to hold you accountable, even though we both know that whatever punishment I give is warranted. I've freely made this choice to send away your sin because I love you."

When we read that we should forgive one another in the same manner in which Christ forgave us (Ephesians 4:32; Colossians 3:13), it means with this free and gracious spirit.

"But," you say with great truth, "she doesn't deserve it!"

That's the whole point. No one *deserves* forgiveness. God chooses to send our sins away in spite of our hearts and our actions.

> He does not treat us as our sins deserve or repay us according to our iniquities. *Psalm 103:10*

We in turn do not treat those who have hurt us as they deserve either. We freely send away their debt.

When my back is bothering me, I am very aware of certain things.

Physically I ache, sometimes to the point of nausea.

Emotionally I'm touchier, more frail, and more self-centered.

Spiritually I wonder why God doesn't heal me—or at least lessen the pain and inconvenience.

When we don't forgive, our spiritual out-of-jointedness causes troublesome consequences, too.

There may be physical reactions like headaches and bad stomachs. David said that when he was in trouble concerning forgiveness, his bones ached and his strength was sapped (Psalm 32:3-4).

Another grave danger of an unforgiving spirit is that we become vulnerable to emotions like anger and bitterness. We develop judgmental attitudes and critical spirits.

Spiritually, an unforgiving heart cannot have the close fellowship with God that both he and we desire. And if we don't forgive, Paul states boldly, we give Satan the opportunity to outwit us (2 Corinthians 2:10-11).

On the contrary, when we do forgive, we have the freedom that comes with obedience to the will of God.

We're free:

- from old hurts and bitternesses
- to forget what's behind and press on to the future
- to fill with love and acceptance the space that hatred and anger formerly occupied
- of the control the hated person had over us as long as we wouldn't forgive

It's natural to try to hold on to anger and hurt. It's understandable. But the Bible clearly says it's not right. We must choose whether we want to behave naturally or become godly.

When I was a kid I went to church with the family down the street. I'd rather have gone with my family, but they had no interest in attending.

I can remember thinking, "If Mom really loved me, she'd come to church with me."

But she never did, and I still knew she loved me. From this situation I learned two important truths about relationships and forgiveness.

First, I became aware that *there are many ways to say, "I love you," and we must allow family and friends to say it in their own ways.* Mom didn't go to church with me, but she drove me and my friends everywhere. She sat up half the night talking with me. And she did without so that I might have.

I can become bitter and angry because she didn't define love as I did. Or, I can accept that by her definition and by her intent, she was a loving mother. It seems to me that choosing the second option is the only way that makes sense.

Now that I have two grown sons, I sometimes wonder how they think I should have defined love and didn't. What hurts are they dealing with because I couldn't be what they wanted?

Sometimes we simply couldn't satisfy both boys. When we showed our love to Chip and let his band play in the basement for his high-school years, were we showing a lack of love to Jeff who wanted them out so he could have peace and quiet? If Jeff wanted to, he could say we didn't love him because we didn't define love *his* way.

But forgiveness means that we accept the fact that our parents tried. They might not have succeeded all the time, but they tried. After all, how many parents look at their newborn and declare, "My goal for this child is to make her life as miserable as I can"?

All parents fail, but the great majority try. They are limited by their backgrounds, their training, their experiences, their personalities, but they try. Let's all of us adult children forgive the hurts that arise because they and we defined love differently. Let's send away the anger and the resentment and forgive our parents as Christ has forgiven us.

The second thing I learned about forgiveness and relationships is that ***unfulfilled expectations or unrealized ideals can cause great anger.***

I wanted my mom to be the perfect Christian mother. I wanted her to be Mrs. Auffort or Mrs. Haven or Mrs. Cairns. Instead she was Mrs. Gordinier; she was herself.

Sometimes it's hard to forgive moms and dads, brothers and sisters, husbands and children for being themselves.

"Shape up!" we want to shout. "Go to church! Get a better job! Stop trying to control me! Keep your opinions to yourself! Lose fifty pounds! Pay attention for once!"

When I was a teen-ager and would go shopping with Mom, she liked to hold my hand as we walked. Talk about embarrassing! I thought I'd die.

Such embarrassment is very typical of teens because they suffer terribly when parents are unique instead of perfect. Some of us grow to adulthood still seeking perfect parents. It's time to acknowledge that such creatures don't exist and never will.

> Be kind and compassionate to one another, forgiving each other, just as in Christ God forgave you. *Ephesians 4:32*

There are some of you reading this section with anger.

Give me a break! you're saying. *Who gets upset about church or no church, holding hands or not holding hands? You don't know what real hurt is!*

Your mother was never passed out on the sofa, bottle on the floor beside her, when you brought a friend over.

Your father didn't have trouble keeping his hands off your daughter.

Your husband didn't leave you for another woman.

Your child didn't tell terrible lies about you, lies everybody believed no matter what you said or did.

I don't want to hear about forgiveness. You haven't the right to talk about it.

In one sense I acknowledge your point. I have known none of this pain and therefore don't fully comprehend the difficulties and realities of forgiveness.

In another sense I challenge your faulty reasoning. It's not I who says you have to forgive. It's God. I am merely repeating what he has said many times over.

As I write this I am vacationing with my family on a Canadian lake that Chuck has been coming to since he was ten. It's gorgeous and wonderfully rustic, though rustic in this case means no indoor plumbing.

Earlier today I stood hip deep in this lake, spring-fed and frigid. I couldn't bring myself to get completely wet, so to wash my hair, I bent at the waist and stuck my head in the water.

As I was in this awkward position rinsing my hair, I was struck with how interesting the shoreline was upside down, especially the car in the front yard a few cabins east. It was draped with one of those tan covers that protect the entire vehicle from the weather.

Why in the world, I wondered, *does someone have a covered car in the front yard of their lakeside cabin? Sort of kills the ambiance.*

When I straightened up, I looked again and quickly realized my error. It wasn't a covered car in the front yard; it was a covered motor boat tied to their dock.

When we as humans look at forgiveness, we look at the issue upside down and consequently misinterpret what we see. But when we look at this very difficult topic from God's viewpoint, the car becomes a boat, so to speak.

- We give people absolution they don't deserve because Christ absolved our sin.
- We send away hurts we have every right to harbor because God sent away our sin.

- We freely forgive rather than try to get even because God in Christ has freely forgiven us.

It should be noted that being a forgiver does not mean being a patsy or a pushover or a weak person.

- A woman can forgive but still work to change the circumstances that have involved her daughter in drugs.
  "I will not give you any money, Dana, but I'll be glad to go to the mall with you and pay for your purchases."
- A man can forgive but still not allow himself to continue to be manipulated.
  "I do love you, Mom, but we are having Christmas at our own home this year. I'm sorry if this makes you cry, but we've made this choice."
- A woman can forgive but not allow opportunity for sin to continue.
  "Tom, I want to tell you now while you're calm that the next time you verbally attack me, I'm taking the kids and leaving the house for the evening. I will not allow you to speak to me that way."
- A man can forgive but let people deal with the consequences of their own acts.
  "Chaz, you wrecked the car. You have to pay for the insurance increase. If you lose half your summer salary to make the payment, that's life, kid."

Enough of theory. Let's get as concrete as we can, as one-two-three as possible. What do we do when there is someone we must forgive?

I think we must begin with ourselves and acknowledge our unforgiving spirits as sin.

> "Why do you look at the speck of sawdust in your brother's eye and pay no attention to the plank in your own eye? How can you say to your brother, 'Let me take the speck out of your eye,' when all the time there is a plank in your own eye? You hypocrite, first take the plank out of your own eye, and then you will see clearly to remove the speck from your brother's eye." *Matthew 7:3-5*

Next, we must give the offenses against us, no matter how big or small, to God to bear and to heal. We've held on to them much too long.

God, the pain of my unforgiving heart has been eating me alive for years. I no longer want to bear it. I have been wrong to hold on to it this long. I give it to you. Please take it. Please heal my heart.

If you are a visual person, imagine handing this hurt to God. If you're a concrete person, write the offenses on a piece of paper and offer it to God as a sacrifice by actually burning it.

What we are doing is sending away both the offense against us and our right to be hurt by it. We are letting go of what is a *natural* response for what is a *godly* response.

Our forgiving is both an instantaneous thing and a process. There is a moment of great decision when we acknowledge that we will send the offense away. Then come the thousands of other moments when we remind ourselves that we have chosen forgiveness, moments when our minds bring back the hurts.

These many moments don't mean our choice to forgive wasn't effective. It means we are human forgivers, in process but not yet perfect.

We often hear the phrase about forgiving but not forgetting. Let's think about this idea in relation to our Model of forgiving, God.

The writer of Hebrews, quoting Jeremiah, speaks of God forgiving Israel's sin. He "will remember their sins no more" (Hebrews 8:12). Here we have the essence of forgiving—remembering no more.

God knows everything, including our sin. Because he's God, he can't forget it. Rather he sends it away; he remembers it no more. So it must be with us. We must not remember the sins against us.

Because forgiving is a process, we tell ourselves with frequency, "Don't recall that!" However, if all we try to do is not remember, we will leave a void in our thoughts and emotions where the pain and bitterness used to be. It's a rule of physics that vacuums cannot exist; something will fill the hole. Because we're used to our unforgiving spirit, that's what will rush back in *unless we have an alternative.*

> Finally, brothers, whatever is true, whatever is noble, whatever is right, whatever is pure, whatever is lovely, whatever is admirable—if anything is excellent or praiseworthy—think about such things. *Philippians 4:8*

We must fill our minds with the promises of God, with Christian music, with good books, with memories of good times, with the lovely, pure, and right things.

It's hard to quote over and over "I will never leave you nor forsake you" when all we've remembered for years is being deserted, but we can choose to do so.

It's hard to turn on Christian music and make a joyful noise to the Lord when all we recall is being belittled, but we can learn to do so.

Just because something is hard doesn't mean it's impossible. It just means it's hard. We are in process, and in the strength of the Spirit we can change. We can become godly. We can put off hurt, anger, resentment, and poor-little-me thinking. We can forgive.

Summary

Forgiving is sending away both the affront against us and the right to extract payment for it, and doing so in the gracious spirit of the Lord.

There are negative physical, emotional, and spiritual consequences when we don't forgive and great freedom when we do.

People give love differently, and we must forgive parents who defined love differently than we did. We must also forgive them for not being perfect. Forgiving is not a sign of weakness.

We start by acknowledging our own unforgiving hearts as sinful. Then we give the offense to God and choose not to dwell on it. Rather we think about lovely, pure, and right things. We also realize forgiving is a process.

QUESTIONS, QUESTIONS . . .

1. How should we relate to the person who chronically delights in hurting, offending and/or taking advantage?
   - Matthew 18:21-22
   - Luke 17:4
   - Colossians 3:13

2. How do you respond to the person who says, "You don't know what was done to me! They don't deserve to be forgiven"?
   - 1 Peter 3:18
   - Ephesians 2:4-5
   - Philippians 3:13-14

3. What does Scripture reply to someone who says, "But they're getting away with great wrongs! How can I forgive when I know the hurt they've given?"
   - Galatians 6:7-9
   - 1 Corinthians 4:4-5

4. Is forgiving excusing? Do I condone when I forgive?
   - John 8:10-11

5. Read Exodus 20:5-6. The modern terms for suffering from the sins of the fathers are "dysfunctional" and "codependent." Are we locked into our past? Is there no cure? Read 2 Corinthians 5:17.

5

caring = accepting one another

♥

"OKAY, CHUCK," I SAID, TAKING A DEEP BREATH AND SQUARING my shoulders. "Tell me two things you accept about me—which means you'd change them if you could, but you can't."

Offering such an opening to someone is asking for it, but I was willing to risk all for the sake of this book.

"Well," he said thoughtfully. *Was he trying to figure out how to be kind,* I wondered, *or were there so many things that he'd like to change that he was having trouble choosing only two?* "One thing I accept is your weight."

I knew he'd say that. He still weighs the same as when we married. I, on the other hand, have acquired what is kindly called a "matronly figure."

One time when we were discussing my weight, Chuck said, "I've concluded that if you're ever thin again, you'll probably be sick. So I guess your weight is better."

Well, I'd like to be thin again, too, but not at the cost of my health or my personality.

"Okay," I said to Chuck. "What else do you accept about me?"
"Your tendency to finish sentences for me."

I expected this comment, too. I do tend to finish his sentences for him, especially in the adrenaline flow of a good discussion or social occasion. I've been a teacher, a counselor, a mother, a speaker, and a writer, and it's hard not to jump right in when I think I see where the sentence is going.

Besides, one of the things I have to work on accepting about Chuck is his deliberateness. He does everything thoroughly and carefully. He always turns off all the lights. He always locks the car. He's always on time. He always balances his checkbook. And he likes to finish his sentences.

> We who are strong ought to bear with the failings of the weak and not to please ourselves. Each of us should please his neighbor for his good, to build him up. Accept one another, then, just as Christ accepted you, in order to bring praise to God. *Romans 15:1-2, 7*

The Roman Christians were a varied bunch, which is an understatement tantamount to saying it gets chilly at the Arctic Circle in winter. Rich, poor; citizen, slave; Jew, Gentile; male, female; wise, foolish; strong, weak.

In short, they were a bit like we are.

One way to tie all these disparate personalities and backgrounds together, Paul notes, is to accept one another. Christ accepts us all, and as always, his example models what should be our pattern.

Accepting goes far beyond merely putting up with. It means receiving someone to ourselves without promise of a favorable reception in return. In other words, I should accept Sally even though I know that she may not respond to me in what *I think is a proper manner.* I must learn to be satisfied with her in spite of the holes I see. (I'm not talking about holes caused by what the Bible calls sin. We'll talk more about that problem later.)

Learning to accept one another requires developing certain thought patterns.

- We learn to give up our expectations.
- We stop projecting our thoughts onto others.
- And we come to recognize the flip side of the characteristics that bother us.

Expectations

It is very easy to look for specific, desired actions from those we love and deal with—things we feel are our due.

I'm not talking about societal expectations like the head of a household earning a wage to care for that household, or everyone stopping for stop signs, or students doing their homework. I'm talking about personal agendas we write for other people, agendas that at close scrutiny often are mainly for our own benefit.

These expectations may be for fine things. It's the *expecting* of them, the subtle requiring of them, that's the problem.

Irene has a romantic heart and assumes Pat, her new husband, does, too. She expects flowers for her birthday and expensive dinners for their anniversaries.

"Loving husbands do that for their wives," she says, putting down the romance novel she's reading.

Tom keeps moving from church to church, leaving each with great disappointment after a year or so.

"The pastor just didn't feed me," he always says. "I learn so much from ——," and he names his favorite radio teacher. "Don't I have a right to expect as much from my personal pastor?"

Adrienne has a fourteen-year-old daughter whose room is a disaster, whose disposition is erratic, whose Christian commitment is minimal, and whose mouth is in constant motion.

"I'm so disappointed with her," Adrienne says. "I expected so much more after all we've done for her."

Brenda witnessed a minor family fracas in a church parking lot and was very distressed. "You should have seen her, yelling at her kid like that. And he sassed her right back! Every time I think I've found a believer I can count on to be consistent, something like this happens. I'm so disenchanted with Christians."

When we, like these people, saddle others with our personal expectations, expectations they frequently know nothing about, we open ourselves to constant disappointment. No one ever seems to live up to the ideals we set. Our hopes and dreams are constantly being dashed on the rocky shores of bitter reality.

> Accept one another, then, just as Christ accepted you, in order to bring praise to God. *Romans 15:7*

Irene must accept Pat, flowers or no, allowing him time to learn to be her husband, especially since she is completely different from his mother and sisters.

Tom needs to accept his pastor, realizing he is God's man just as much as the radio teacher—even if his talents aren't as prodigious.

Adrienne needs to accept her daughter, understanding that she's right on schedule for maturity. Fourteen eventually becomes twenty-four.

Brenda needs to accept her Christian friend, remembering that she, too, has bad days.

Such yielding of expectations enables us to deal successfully with people *where they are at the moment*. It allows for process and progress and growing in the Lord. It enables us to enjoy every forward step another takes and gives us an understanding spirit when someone proves he or she is all too human. And above all, it keeps us focused on the Lord for our fulfillment and satisfaction.

Projection

Where expectation centers on what we desire people to do for us, projection involves ascribing to others our ideas and emotions. We know how they are feeling and what they are thinking because we put our assumptions and conclusions on them.

There is a story about a man who had a flat tire on a country road at dusk. He opened his trunk to get out his spare, only to discover that he had no lug wrench with him.

Ah, he remembered, *I passed a house not too long ago. I'll just walk back there and ask to borrow their wrench.*

He set off hopefully. As he walked, a series of thoughts crossed his mind.

I hope they're not eating dinner. I'd hate to disturb them then because they might get upset. No one likes cold food.

No, they won't be upset. They'll be mad. The man will answer the door already angry, and he won't want to help me. And why should he help me anyway? After all, he's got this foul temper and I'm just a stranger. He'll probably laugh in my face and tell me about the service station ten miles down the road.

What a nasty man! What right has he to treat me this way?

Our hero rang the doorbell, and a man answered.

"Yes?" he said. "How can I help you?"

"Just give me your blankety-blank wrench!"

Projection—putting our assumptions and conclusions on the other guy.

It is true that certain aspects of personality are predictable, and we plan accordingly. This isn't projection. Chuck, for example, likes lots of notice about things, so I know not to suggest going out to dinner at the last minute. I'm not putting my conclusions on him. I'm acknowledging a specific, well-verified aspect of his personality.

When I speak of projection, I'm talking about assuming to understand another's mind, another's motives, another's intent, often in spite of what they say.

Lainie came to me for counsel and said, "My husband doesn't love me."

"How do you know that?" I asked. "Did he tell you?"

"Oh, no. He'd never tell me that. He wouldn't want to hurt me. I just know."

"How? How do you know? Doesn't he come home anymore after work? Doesn't he spend time with you and the kids?"

"Oh, he's there just as much as usual."

"Then doesn't he talk to you? Does he pull away and just watch TV? Doesn't he want to go to bed with you anymore?"

"Oh, no. He's with me as much as always, maybe more—though that's just his cover."

"Does he criticize you or belittle you? What makes you so sure he doesn't love you anymore?"

"I just know it."

How can the poor guy ever win? How can he ever convince her of his affection? She assumes to know his mind better than he knows it himself. She is putting her own erroneous conclusions on him and calling them truth.

We all have some tendency to assume we know what the other guy's thinking. That's why the writer of Proverbs warns us, "He who answers before listening—that is his folly and his shame" (Proverbs 18:13).

When we see a man on the street with a red nose, we project a reason for that nose on the man.

- He's an alcoholic.
- He just got punched.
- He has a bad cold.
- He suffers from a skin condition.
- He spent yesterday at the beach.

Any or all or none of these things may be true. But our tendency will be to assume at least one of the above reasons.

If we come from a family of drinkers, we'll assume alcohol. If our psoriasis is acting up, we'll assume skin condition. If we just returned from the shore and are peeling most unattractively, we'll assume a day at the beach.

> Accept one another, then, just as Christ accepted you, in order to bring praise to God. *Romans 15:7*

We must stop the habit of projecting our thoughts and conclusions onto another. We need to accept each person as he or she is. We must take her at her word until there is specific proof that she is not worthy of trust. We must refrain from analyzing his holes and assuming we understand why these problems exist.

Paul comments that it is the Lord who will bring to light what is hidden and expose the motives of people's hearts (1 Corinthians 4:5). We are not to judge such personal motivations. More bluntly put, we are not to assume the role of the Holy Spirit in another's life. We are to accept each other and allow room for process.

The Flip Side

Remember my comments about how methodical Chuck is and how it drives me crazy sometimes? Interestingly this quality is also one of the things I value most in him. He may unplug my curling iron when I think it's heating up or turn lights off while I'm still in the room, but he also always pays the bills, keeps the cars running smoothly, sees that we give regularly to church, and changes the batteries in the fire alarms.

It is this 1-2-3, neatness-counts reliability that makes him such a good research engineer and trouble-shooter as well as a wonderful husband and father. His boss knows he'll show up every morning. We know he'll come home every evening. The pastor knows he'll fulfill any responsibilities he accepts.

I have a choice when I look at Chuck. I can get all upset when he leaves me in the dark, or I can yell, "Lights, please!" and thank God for how consistent he is. I can learn to appreciate the flip side of being methodical.

Remember how I finish Chuck's sentences, even though I try not to? Chuck can center on this frustrating characteristic of mine, or he can look at its flip side.

Not too long ago he said, "I think you are just the right wife for me. If I didn't have you, I'd be rigid. You lighten me up and help me be spontaneous."

And occasionally drive him crazy in the process.

I've found that learning to look for the flip side of irritating characteristics frees both parties. There's freedom from being aggravated and freedom from knowing you aggravate. Also a new sense of appreciating each other and being appreciated blossoms.

Such acceptance does not automatically preclude prayer about the habit or characteristic that troubles us. Nor does it mean we can't speak about the problem. It merely means we can neither demand nor expect change.

It's important that Chuck has told me it bothers him that I finish his sentences. Now I am aware and will work at stopping that action as a matter of common courtesy and Christian love. After all, I don't want him to feel he has to stay away from me at parties because I interrupt him too much.

It's also important for him to learn that lights left on don't signify the end of the world. Infidelity, embezzlement, and heresy are worth great anguish, not 60 watt bulbs—or even 100s.

But I know, and so does he, that no matter how often I pray, "Set a watch, O Lord, before my lips," I will fail. I'll take over his story or finish his sentence.

And no matter how hard he tries, he'll turn off the lights and say, "Do you leave them on just to aggravate me?"

Accept one another. There is no other practical way to deal with our quirks and failings. Accept one another in Christ to bring praise to God.

Summary

Accepting one another is receiving each other and being satisfied with each other despite the holes we see.

We need to lay aside expectations, things we want from others.

We need to lay aside projections, assumptions, and conclusions we place on others based on our thoughts.

We need to see the flip side of the aggravating characteristics of others.

We do all this after the model of Christ to the praise of God.

Questions, Questions . . .

1. Are there people in your life who you feel do not accept you? What is the emotional consequence of their attitude toward you? The spiritual consequence? What is your responsibility toward them?
   - Colossians 3:13 *Forgiving one another*
   - John 15:12 *Love one another as I have loved you.*

2. Do you have expectations about the people in your life? What are they? Are you willing to let them go? What should be our heart attitude and our goal as we yield our expectations?
   - Philippians 2:14-16 *Do all things without grumbling or disputings*
   - Romans 14:1 *Accept the one who is weak in faith but not for the purpose of judgment.*

3. What are the dangers in assuming we know the motives of someone's heart?
   - 1 Samuel 16:7 *man looks at outward appearance God looks at the heart*
   - 1 Corinthians 2:11 *Who knows the thoughts of a man except the spirit of the man*
   - 1 Corinthians 4:4-6 *When the Lord comes he will disclose what is in the hearts of men.*
   - 1 Corinthians 8:2-3 *If anyone knows God, he is known by him.*

4. Many people establish friendships and marriages built on the characteristics they lack but see and admire in the other. In time these are the very characteristics that drive wedges. What is the biblical way to deal with these wedges?
   - Romans 14:13 *Let us not judge one another but determine not to put a stumbling block in a brother's way.*
   - Romans 15:5 *Give perseverance & encouragement to others as God has to you*
   - 1 Corinthians 13:4-7 *Love is patient, kind — does not seek his own, does not brag, is not arrogant. Rejoices with the truth.*

6

caring = admonishing one another

IF THERE IS ANYTHING IN THE WORLD GUARANTEED TO KEEP ONE humble, it's children, especially one's own.

As a homeroom mother for Chip's first grade, I helped organize and put on their Halloween party. It was sort of fun.

When we got home afterwards, I asked Chip how he liked it.

"The party was okay, Mom, but you weren't." He wasn't being nasty. He was stating the fact as he saw it.

"I wasn't?" I was quite surprised. I thought things had gone quite well even if my corn popper didn't pop and the kids never got their expected popcorn. They'd certainly had enough else. "What was wrong?"

"You talked to everybody dumb. You talked to them like they were babies. They're not babies. They're in first grade."

Slightly taken aback, I tried to defend myself. (Don't we always?) "I didn't think the kids seemed that upset."

Chip snorted. Obviously I wouldn't know an upset first-grader if I saw one.

"Know those pumpkins we made? The ones from paper bags? Know when we had to paste the faces on? You kept saying, 'Good work. You do good pasting.' Of course they do good pasting. Anybody can do good pasting! It was dumb to say it."

The whole time he was talking, still very politely, I kept thinking that this criticism wasn't supposed to start until he was a teen-ager.

"When I go to school again, the kids are going to tell me what a weird mother I have." He looked like he had a great burden to bear, but somehow he'd manage.

"Do me a favor," I asked. "Don't suggest to them that I'm weird. Wait and see if they mention it first." No use prejudicing them unnecessarily.[1]

I wrote this years ago, and it reminds me of the fact that everybody likes to give advice and correction, no matter how young or old. Many times the issues involved are no more important than paper pumpkins or elbows on the table or how large the tip should be. Many times the issues are very serious.

When I was twenty-six, I had to have a total hysterectomy, and as a result, both our boys are adopted. I count us fortunate to have them and have had relatively few problems with not bearing my own children.

There was one time, however, when I had great difficulty. My friend Hannah became pregnant and showed absolutely no emotion. She wasn't happy. She wasn't sad. She wasn't anything.

For some reason, this lack of visible reaction ate at me. I understood joy at conception. I even understood consternation, especially among older friends who had thought their families complete years ago. But nothing!

I groused about Hannah's lack of feeling. I pondered it as I cared for my own little boys, and in my mind it grew more and more outrageous and incomprehensible.

One day our family was in the car. Chuck and Chip were in the front seat, and baby Jeff and I were in the back. I was, as usual in those days, complaining about Hannah.

We stopped for a red light and Chuck looked at me in the rearview mirror.

"Gayle," he said calmly, "I don't know if you realize it, but you are letting this situation make you very bitter and critical. You'd better be careful."

The light changed and his attention returned to the road. I sat and stared at the back of his head and knew he was absolutely right.

What business of mine was it whether Hannah was excited or not? If I were honest, she was merely acting in character. Nothing visibly ruffled her—not marriages, not jobs, not pregnancies. Besides, her husband seemed perfectly happy with her response. Who was I to be finding fault? What colossal, sinful nerve!

There are two points to be noted in this story. First, I was wrong in finding fault. Secondly, Chuck was correct in finding fault.

What makes the difference?

First, I was being critical over something that was merely a personality characteristic. Hannah didn't jump up and down like I thought she should. Big deal. Chuck, on the other hand, commented on something that the Bible specifically calls sin—the critical and nasty spirit I was developing.

Second, I never did speak to Hannah about the perceived problem. I just groused behind her back. In contrast, Chuck spoke directly to me about my behavior.

> Let the word of Christ dwell in you richly as you teach and *admonish one another* with all wisdom, and as you sing psalms, hymns and spiritual songs with gratitude in your hearts to God. *Colossians 3:16, italics mine*

Admonish means to put in someone's mind or to warn someone (as opposed to *teach,* which means to impart a positive truth). A problem of some kind exists, and the one creating the problem must be told. She must be warned about the difficulties she's causing, the tensions her activities are generating, the dishonor she's bringing to the name of Christ.

When Chip told me I spoke to his friends unacceptably, he was admonishing me on his level. When Chuck looked me in the eye and said, "Yo, Gayle," he gave me a warning I badly needed.

Because Chip's comments were based on the wisdom of a six-year-old, I felt free to ignore them. I went back over the day in my mind and decided he had over-reacted.

Because Chuck's comments were based on the Word of God and its standards, I had no such freedom. If I wanted to be the Christian I claimed to be, I had to listen to that warning.

The potential for hurt and misunderstanding involved in admonishing makes it critical that a corrector dwell in the Word. Equally important is the fact that the admonishment itself should be based on the Word, not mere opinion. *Let the word of Christ dwell in you richly as you teach and admonish one another with all wisdom.*

How could I argue with Chuck when I knew him to be a man of the Word? When I knew him to be basing his comments to me on the standards of the Word, not merely his personal opinion?

I did at least listen to both the admonishments, though, for several reasons:

1. Both Chip and Chuck, by their interest in me and affection for me, had earned the right to point out my flaws.
2. Both Chip and Chuck pointed out my problems in a nonthreatening voice, so that I didn't become too defensive to learn or too hurt to hear.
3. Both Chip and Chuck made a logical argument based on the problem as they saw it, and they didn't attack my entire person.
4. Neither Chip nor Chuck admonished me frequently so that when they did say something of this sort, I knew it was important to listen and to search for the kernel of truth in their comments.

Solomon knew about admonition when he wrote, "Wounds from a friend can be trusted" (Proverbs 27:6).

When I taught junior-high school, the mother of a lovely seventh-grader who was fast going out of control both in school and out came to school for a conference.

"Linda needs to study," I told the mother. "She's smart, but she's not doing any of her work. Her grades are getting worse and worse."

Her mother nodded. "She likes to go out at night, and when she gets home, it's late and she goes right to bed."

"You let her stay out late on school nights? But she's only twelve."

"She cries if I don't let her," said the worried mother, "and I can't stand to see her sad."

Admonishment was what Linda needed, but she wasn't going to get it from her mother because it was an emotionally wrenching thing to do. Those of us who are like Linda's mom and hate confrontation suffer from what has been called "hassle-avoidance."[2] We need to remember that admonition is a command of Scripture. It must be done.

Those of us who feel like tying Linda to her bed and lecturing her for a few hours need to remember that while admonition is a command, it is to be done by one in whom the Word dwells richly. And it is to be done with wisdom.

Let no unwholesome word come out of your mouth, said Paul, but only what builds up the listener (Ephesians 4:29, my translation). Admonishment in this vein is a gift. I pray I'm always fortunate enough to have people in my life of the calibre who care enough to confront me when necessary.

Summary

An admonishment is a calling to one's attention, a warning of a problem.

Admonishers should be dwelling in the Word and the admonition should be based on the Word.

"The wounds of a friend can be trusted," and they must be delivered in a way that will build up, not tear down.

Questions, Questions . . .

1. If someone admonishes us, how should we react?
   - Proverbs 9:8-9
   - Proverbs 15:5

2. Read Galatians 6:1-2. What qualifications are presented here of one who is spiritually mature enough to be used of God? Where do you see yourself in reference to these characteristics?

3. The Bible says we shouldn't judge; we should mind our own business. After all, we have beams in our own eyes. How then can we justify admonishing?

4. Read 1 Peter 4:8. How does the principle in this verse fit in with the principle of admonishing?

7

caring = serving one another

"OKAY," I SAID TO MY THIRD-GRADE SUNDAY-SCHOOL CLASS, "let's go to the table and do some written work."

The kids exploded from their seats and rushed for the table. Unfortunately for the poor kid bringing me the offering basket, he was going against the tide. Both he and the basket went flying.

"Money!" yelled some mercenary soul.

"Look!" yelled others as they watched some coins roll across the floor on their edges.

"Are you okay?" I asked Kenny as he lay on the floor.

He nodded, and I stretched out my hand and hauled him up.

"Let's help Kenny pick the money up," I said and reached for some dimes.

Everybody chased quarters, dimes and nickels cooperatively except Angela. I noticed her sitting at the table, earnestly writing something on her worksheet.

When the money was back in the basket and everyone in their seats, I eased myself down next to Angela.

"What are you writing so seriously?" I asked, curious.

"Nothing," she said, smiling without guile. "I just know that if you look busy when there's a job to be done, you can get out of it."

I haven't seen Angela since she was in third grade twenty-five years ago, though I've often wondered about her. If she hasn't changed, she has the attitude of many Americans.

If I can get out of it, I will.

> You, my brothers, were called to be free. But do not use your freedom to indulge the sinful nature; rather, serve one another in love. *Galatians 5:13*

To serve people means to wait on them, to minister to them, to attend to them. They are the ones having the five-course dinner and you are the waitress bringing it—only you will get no tip.

God does not force us to serve either him or each other. He once again teaches us through the example of Christ.

> Who, being in very nature God,
>   did not consider equality with God
>   something to be grasped,
> but made himself nothing,
>   taking the very nature of a *servant*,
>   being made in human likeness.
> *Philippians 2:6-7, italics mine*

When Christ became our servant, he lowered himself. He gave up his position, the respect that was rightly his, the power that was rightly his. He left all the splendors of glory and came here.

And he did it by choice.

> Your attitude should be the same as that of Christ Jesus.
> *Philippians 2:5*

Like him, we should also become servants of one another by choice, for there is great strength and freedom found in choosing to serve.

We find freedom from futility when we become servants in the name of Jesus. We have a purpose, a reason for living. Our goal is to help, to minister, to lift up, to put ourselves out for the sake of another.

We also find freedom from failure when we choose to serve. We don't have to prove anything because our goal is not achievement but service.

We had the privilege of being part of a new congregation some years ago. We rented the second floor of the recently constructed municipal building for our church, and it proved very satisfactory.

One Sunday Chuck, the boys, and I got there earlier than usual, and we found our pastor sweeping up hundreds of dead flies.

"Where'd they come from?" I asked.

"New buildings are always fly cemeteries," the pastor answered.

"It's funny they were never here before," I said.

Chuck and the pastor both looked at me with an expression that makes you very quickly review what you just said to find out why it was so dumb.

who cares?

"Oh! They have been here!" I looked at my pastor. "Do you come early every Sunday to sweep them up?"

Obviously the answer was yes.

Certainly sweeping up flies every Sunday morning could be called futile or foolish or at the very least unexciting. But because the pastor chose to be a servant, he was free from these negative feelings. He had a purpose with those flies—to allow his congregation to come to a clean place to worship. He was free from futility, even doing grunt labor.

But the man had a masters in theology and was then working on his Ph.D. Wasn't sweeping flies a bit beneath one of his education and position? Wasn't he afraid of being seen as a failure?

When he chose to serve, the pastor freed himself from the fear of being perceived as a failure. He and God understood his motives, and if any person was dense enough to judge him wrongly, the problem was that person's, not the pastor's.

One of the most fascinating things about the fly story is that I never would have known about it at all if we hadn't come early that Sunday. The pastor told no one. He merely served.

You know, Lord, how I serve You
With great emotional fervor
In the limelight.
You know how eagerly I speak for You
At a women's club.
You know how I effervesce when I promote
A fellowship group.

You know my genuine enthusiasm
At a Bible study.

But how would I react, I wonder
If you pointed to a basin of water
And asked me to wash the calloused feet
Of a bent and wrinkled old woman
Day after day
Month after month
In a room where nobody saw
And nobody cared.[1]

Being a footwasher or a fly sweeper is not easy. There's something about the humbleness of the jobs that bothers us. We crave recognition and position. At least, I know *I* do, and I doubt I'm very different from you.

But God doesn't tell us to seek position and praise. He tells us to seek servanthood.

"I became a servant of this gospel by the gift of God's grace," wrote Paul (Ephesians 3:7).

Paul *became* a servant of the gospel. He didn't start out as one. He spent years becoming, relegated to the desert much as Moses was. There, where nobody saw and nobody cared, the Holy Spirit prepared him and taught him.

Through prayer and the power of the Holy Spirit in our lives, we can become servants, too. God's grace is ours as well as Paul's, and we can learn to give up our personal freedom for servanthood just as he did. We are, after all, in process just as he was.

If we are willing to become servants, we must ask God to remake our thinking and give us certain mental attitudes.

- *We must become **available**.*

"Lord, here I am. Use me when and where you see fit."

As we become available to the Lord as servants, we will develop eyes that see the needs around us, and we will be willing to help meet those needs.

- *We must be **humble**, willing to start at the bottom.*

If a friend with three little boys is ill, are we willing to clean her house for her, even the bathroom?

If the bulletins for Sunday need to be folded, are we willing to fold them, even though they refused to print our poem on the back?

Are we willing to be Indians instead of chiefs, even when we know we would be better chiefs than the present ones?

I have prayed for my sons that they learn the truth of the bottom before God blesses them with whatever success he has for them in life. If we won't serve at the bottom, we aren't worthy to serve at the top.

- *We must understand servanthood as a **privilege**.*

We are *allowed* to serve in Jesus' name. He doesn't need us to accomplish his will, but he has chosen to let us help. What a wonderful courtesy! What a wonderful kindness!

It is my privilege to pay your heating bill.

I am fortunate enough to sit with you through the night as you wait at the hospital for word about your son's illness.

I am allowed to clean the church this week for Jesus' sake.

- *We must be willing **to receive** the services of others, knowing their heart is to serve God, too.*

It's easy to get proud when someone tries to help. When I returned once from a week-long writers conference, two friends brought dinner in for us the first two days I was home. My automatic reaction was that I didn't need such help! I might be weary and emotionally spent, but I could manage.

But their ministry of love was so refreshing! All they wanted to do was serve God by serving me, and I almost denied them this joy and myself the encouragement.

Okay, so we should serve. How do we know what is the best way for us to do so?

My first suggestion is that we each do something that fits our unique personalities. What do we like to do? What do we do well? What gives us satisfaction? Our imagination is our only limit.

We must ask ourselves the following questions:

1. What do I dream of doing as service? What sparks me? When I talk, what gets me excited?
2. What needs do I see going unmet? What holes do I ache over in the ministry of my church? What dikes can I plug with my finger?

In my opinion, anyone who likes little kids and enjoys teaching them is worth his or her weight in gold. What a joy to help little ones learn to love God.

But what if I dislike little kids, and I don't want to teach? When I go into someone's home, am I immediately at home in the kitchen? How about the church's kitchen? I could get involved there. I could cater dinners. I could clean up messes. I could be like my friend Josie who says she's served so many church dinners, she figures she's being prepared to work the Marriage Feast of the Lamb.

Hate kitchens? How about smiling? Am I good at that? I could be a greeter Sunday mornings or work in the information booth. I could shake hands after the services. If there's no official committee to oversee these jobs, I can still do it on my own.

Shy? Scared of new people? I could volunteer in the church office. There's always more work in the office than the secretaries can get done. Or I could volunteer to do custodial work. Or to visit the shut-ins.

And if I like dramatic things, I could form a drama team. We could put on skits wherever someone will let us. Or I could start a puppet ministry, either alone or with kids working the puppets.

Like music? I could join the choir or organize a quartet or set up an orchestra. I could share my favorite tapes and CDs with friends, especially new believers or discouraged people. I could develop a music library for church.

Got a tin ear but like to organize? I could help plan VBS or set up a library or keep track of the visitation records. I could send the weekly bulletins to the church's college students.

Enjoy electronics? I could volunteer to work with the tape program or the amplification system. I could tape all the messages and set up a tape library.

Maybe athletics are my joy? I could organize or play on teams that compete with other churches. I could get a group together for aerobics, either formally or informally. I could set up a youth sports program.

What about interior decorating? I could volunteer to help families redo their homes for minimal cost. I could specialize in redoing the rooms of those who are ill.

Like to drive? I could get my bus license and be available to drive the kids—or anyone else—on outings. I could take older people to the doctor or the store.

Enjoy teen-agers? I could be a chaperone for socials and open my house for youth activities. I could be a youth sponsor.

Committed to prayer? I could develop a web of missionaries around the world I pray for regularly. I could pray for all the kids in the junior- and senior-high youth program each week. I could pray daily for the pastor and his family. I could organize a prayer chain for church.

Enjoy writing letters? I could encourage people with notes and cards. I could go through the church directory and send everyone a note saying I had prayed for them that day. I could write to prisoners or servicemen and share the Lord. I could develop international pen-pals.

Like needlework? I could make clothes for those I know who are in financial difficulties. I could sew a project to cheer someone who was discouraged. I could make something for each missionary the church sponsored or each new mom and baby in the congregation.

Like artwork? I could make bulletin boards and design advertising materials. I could paint something for the pastor. I could give lessons to a kid who needs time and encouragement.

Gardening? I could care for the church's plantings or provide flowers for the sanctuary each Sunday. I could take bouquets to the homebound or the discouraged.

Sanctified imagination! Whatever you want to do, do it as a *servant*.

It is important to note that there are times in our lives when we are not free to serve as we might prefer. Instead we are bound to serve as the situation requires. Examples of such circumstances would be moms with little kids or sick kids, adults with aged parents, men or women with unbelieving spouses, and people with empty pocketbooks.

My question to all those in holding patterns: what are you doing to prepare yourself while you wait? Now is your desert. What are you becoming?

In time your circumstances will change. If you have proved yourself worthy where no one knew and no one cared, you may well have your chance to serve by doing what you love. God doesn't try to make our lives miserable by working against all the talents and inclinations he has built into us. He is, after all, a wise God.

The problem is ours. We are too itchy to wait for his direction, too proud to start at the bottom, too disdainful of the training process.

Somewhere I read that the definition of an English gentleman is one who uses a butter knife even when he dines alone. The definition of a servant is one who chooses to make God happy by serving even when no one is looking.

Summary

To serve one another is to minister to each other or to wait on each other, and it is something we do by choice.

We become servants; it is a process.

Servants are available, humble, privileged, and receptive.

We serve best by using the talents and inclinations the Lord has given us, though there may be periods of serving to meet a need when we do what we must instead of what we would like to.

caring = serving one another

Questions, Questions . . .

1. Little kids say, "It isn't fair!" How does fairness come into serving one another?
   - Galatians 6:9-10 5:9 23 do not become weary in doing good!
   - 2 Thessalonians 3:13 5:548 never tire of doing what is right.

2. What do you personally find the most difficult about serving?
   Finding time to do all that I want to do

3. How do parents know when serving their families "as unto the Lord" has crossed over the line and has created an I-deserve-all-I-can-get attitude in the kids?
   - Ephesians 6:1-2 obey your parents — honor your father and your mother
   - Proverbs 29:15,17 Importance of discipline
   - Proverbs 22:6 Train a child in the way he should go and he will not turn from it.

4. In the past you may have been taken advantage of as you've served. How can these Scriptures encourage you?
   - Philippians 2:3-11 (5) 15 33 Act with humility; not selfish ambition
   - Colossians 3:23-24

8

caring = submitting to one another

♥

"I'M GOING TO BE PART OF A CONCERT AT WEST CHESTER University," Nancy said. "A friend is giving her masters recital, and I'm helping her out."

"What are you doing?" I asked. "Are you singing together or something?"

"No. She's taking her masters degree in accompanying, so she has to have various artists perform while she plays for them. I'm her vocalist."

Chuck and I went to the concert and found it very interesting. By the very nature of her field, accompaniment, the star of the show was obscured. Her job was to present the other musicians, to follow their leads, to make them look good. In doing so she became essentially invisible even as she sat at her piano in the middle of the stage. Even backstage after the concert, the tendency was to congratulate the obvious performers, not the woman who submitted her talent to theirs, even though it was her night.

> Submit to one another out of reverence for Christ.
> *Ephesians 5:21*

Submitting to another person's will or wishes is one of those Christian character traits that we gag over. We prefer to captain our fates and master our souls, not step aside for someone else.

Yet God asks us to yield to others, just like the accompanist did, just like Jesus did. Jesus submitted to those who mocked him and beat him and killed him. He allowed them to have their way at his expense.

While God doesn't ask us to go to Calvary, he does ask us to look to the interests of others, considering them better than ourselves (Philippians 2:3-4). We are to be the accompanists who make our friends and family look wonderful.

Several years ago when my kids were in Little League, I had an evening in which there were two places I needed to be—a game and a meeting of the planning committee for the next year's women's program. Since I was the Program Chairman (capital letters, roll of the drums), I was important to the meeting. I had a year's worth of programs that looked great to me, especially since they were included in my recently published book called *New Program Ideas For Women's Groups*.

Imagine my great surprise when I arrived at the planning meeting (late because of the baseball game) and found out they had gone on without me, developing another entire program—and a good one at that.

"But I've got my plans right here," I said, flashing my book.

"Mmm," said the president. "I think we already have everything set. Janine had these wonderful ideas and we're going to use them."

Everybody nodded, and the meeting moved to the next topic. I was the only one who wasn't grinning from ear to ear. I was too busy being flabbergasted.

"But I'm the Program Chairman," I wanted to yell. "I've got my programs all set. They're even listed right here in the book I wrote about how to have great women's programs. What do you mean you're going with Janine's ideas?!"

I didn't yell, of course. My mother had raised me better than that. But I thought a lot, and most of my thoughts weren't very edifying.

On the drive home I began to mutter to myself in earnest. The gall of all of them, but especially Janine! She *knew* I was Program Chairman, yet she tramped right into my territory and took over. And all because I was being a good mother and sitting through my umpty-umpth Little League game!

I got home and groused to Chuck, who reacted to the whole situation with the emotion it deserved. He raised an eyebrow. Not at Janine and all the others. Oh, no. At *me*.

Thanks for the support, buddy.

It was while I lay in bed snarling quietly at the ceiling that the Lord tapped me on the shoulder. I don't mean an actual physical touch or voice or anything. I mean he impressed upon me very graciously his view of the whole traumatic event.

Have you ever heard of the concept of submitting to each other?

Certainly.

What does it mean?

You yield to the other guy.

Even Janine?

But I'm Program Chairman!

What's more important? Your chairmanship or the women's fellowship program?

You mean my ego or the women's fellowship program, right?

I understood what the Lord was impressing upon me. I could stay mad and hurt and resentful and destroy any hope of unity and common purpose for the year, or I could submit to Janine and the rest of the board.

I learned a couple of important principles from this situation.

1. The health of the unit is more important than my position or feelings.
2. When I do yield, I should do so with grace, not martyrdom.

I yielded to Janine and organized and carried out her plans for the year. And on most days I was able to be honestly glad that it was a very good year. On the other days, I sought the Lord's help to correct my wrong spirit.

If we are unwilling to yield, to bend to the wishes and opinions of others, we are asserting that we have *all* the answers and the *only* answers. It must be done our way, which is the only way. We are in deep trouble when we see ourselves as this infallible. It is for this reason that some fine Christians are not suited to be elders or deacons. They cannot yield their opinions easily. Their position is more important than the health of the unit. And factionalism flourishes.

"Live in harmony with one another," wrote Paul. "Do not be proud, but be willing to associate with people of low position. Do not be conceited" (Romans 12:16).

It's hard to live in harmony when we're busy protecting our turf. Harmony requires that everyone sing the same song at the same pace and strength, led by the same Director.

My father was a professional musician, but for some reason I never inherited any amount of his talent. My main problem is my ear; I can never be certain that it and my vocal chords will match notes. As a result, I'm strictly a choral singer, much in need *caring = submitting to one another*

of the other voices to keep me where I belong. To open one's mouth and know what note's going to come out must be a marvelous thing.

But there's a lot to be said for choral singing. It teaches cooperation and a yielding of oneself. No one voice should stand out in a choir. The glory is in the oneness of multiple voices, the blending of many notes.

That should also be the glory of any group of Christians: the oneness, the likemindedness. We hold such precious truths in common. We believe in the triune God, the deity of Christ, the authority of the Word. We believe in the efficacy of Christ's atonement for our sins and the need for a personal faith in that atonement.

Certainly there are distinctives within the Body as a whole, as well as each local body. Some are on theological issues like gifts and eternal security. Some are on temporal issues like patterns of worship and dress. But we share Christ, and it's in his name that we submit to one another.

While we, as the martyrs through the centuries, should go to death for the verities of the faith, we must be careful to exercise caution about the distinctives. When the issue is a pattern of thought as opposed to the Object of our faith, we must allow for our variations. As soprano, alto, tenor, and bass do not sing the same notes, neither do believers. It is from the blending of the different notes that harmony comes.

Figuring out how to make submission and harmony work in the choral intricacies of family life is another great challenge. There's no sheet music or hymnal that charts which are his notes and which are hers. When does he give in to her and when does she cede to him? And what about the kids? Should the parents ever yield to them?

To answer the last and easier question first, yes, there are times we yield to the kids.

Arlene took her junior-high daughter shopping for shoes several years ago. They came home with a pair of sandals with the stacked wooden soles that made the wearer a good two inches taller than she actually was. At that time, they were all the rage.

"Why did you ever let her buy those stupid things?" Arlene's husband asked her.

"Because they're only stupid," she answered. "I'd rather save my 'no's for things that really matter."

What a wise attitude Arlene had. To phrase it another way, we need to pick our wars. We want to avoid arguing about insignificant things.

Each of us defines insignificant things differently. To me, neat bedrooms are insignificant, but church attendance isn't. Clothes worn to church aren't worth a war (as long as they are modest—which is scriptural and therefore important) but respect for people is paramount.

It takes a lot of thought to decide what really matters to us, but we need to come to conclusions on the matter. Then, because we know what's important, we know where we can choose to give in. And our kids learn about submission and harmony because they see those principles lived.

Between husband and wife, submitting and living in harmony are a pleasure in direct proportion to the dedication of each to the Lord. It is only our commitment to become Christ-like that makes us willing to say, "If that's what you want, it's okay with me." It's only our decision to live in a godly manner that allows us to say, "I feel strongly about this issue. Let's talk and find a meeting ground. I don't want to hurt you."

As the health of the women's program was more important than my ego, so is the health of the nuclear family more important than an individual member's ego. As I needed to yield to Janine with grace, not martyrdom, so do we need to surrender in our families. We are, after all, on the same team, and the idea is to make the other guy happy.

The one facet of submitting that makes it painless—or relatively so—is that doing it is our choice. No one can make us submit our hearts and spirits against our wills. They can force behavior but no more. We *choose* to submit to each other.

I've noticed that some women who think their husbands hard and unyielding have inadvertently helped create this atmosphere in their homes because they don't express their true feelings. They hedge what they say, thinking disagreement means lack of wifely submission.

They don't say, "I hate it. Please don't buy it." Instead they say, "Whatever you want, dear," while their stomachs are churning and their spirits resentful.

They don't say, "I'd rather not have company Friday night. I'm just too worn out after the work-week. How about Saturday?" They just sigh and ask, "How many?" thinking that being a good wife is really the pits.

The same chapter in Ephesians that says *submit* also says *speak the truth in love.* We mustn't do one without the other.

The end result of submission and harmony is, I think, unity.

> May the God who gives endurance and encouragement give you a spirit of unity among yourselves as you follow Christ Jesus. *Romans 15:5*

When Jesus prayed in the Garden just before going to the cross, he asked the Father that we believers might be one as he and God are one (John 17:20-23). Unity, Christ noted, would be another sign to the world that believers belong to God.

who cares?

When I was first out of college, I lived at home a year before I married. During that year I attended my first congregational business meeting. The general topic under discussion was the renovation of the parsonage, and the specific sticky issue was the kitchen. Some people were adamant about linoleum, some about tiles. If kitchen carpet had existed then, I'm sure there would have been a third faction.

I listened in amazement as people got quite excited. If I hadn't known better, I would have thought that the linoleum and tile salesmen had sent their representatives.

Finally some woman raised her hand, was recognized and stood. In a timid and nervous voice she asked, "Wouldn't it be wise to let the pastor's wife select what she wants in the kitchen? After all, it's hers."

The sheer common sense of the suggestion won the day and unity was restored. But if kitchens can rouse such ire, what about real issues?

When a friend of ours who attended an especially feisty church joked that their next split would be over red or blue carpet in the sanctuary, there was enough truth in his crack to make it bittersweet.

> I appeal to you, brothers, in the name of our Lord Jesus Christ, that all of you agree with one another so that there may be no divisions among you and that you may be perfectly united in mind and thought. *1 Corinthians 1:10*

In and of ourselves we are all opinionated and stubborn people, not ideal choices to model biblical submission and unity.

In and through the power of the Holy Spirit, we can become giving and cooperative, evidence to the world that God has indeed sent a Savior who makes men and women new creations.

Summary

Submitting to one another is much like being a musical accompanist. We must yield ourselves to others for the good of the whole.

The health of the unit is more important than my personal position or opinion.

When I do yield, I must do so with grace, not martyrdom.

While we must stand firm on the verities of the faith, we must learn to appreciate the harmonies of various distinctives.

The end result of submission and harmony is unity, a sign to the world that God has sent Jesus to be our Savior.

who cares?

Questions, Questions . . .

1. Have you faced (or are you facing) situations of disunity or disharmony in your family or in a church? How was (is) the situation (being) handled? Were (are) things (being) done biblically?
   - Matthew 18:15-17
   - Galatians 6:1
   - 1 Peter 4:8

2. We live in a culture that teaches that we deserve personal satisfaction and fulfillment. How does that concept stand up in light of Philippians 2:2-5 and the verses following?

3. Discuss the conflict between what we are and what we are becoming and how it affects unity.
   - Galatians 3:26-28
   - Romans 7:21-25

4. You have submitted and are trying to live in harmony, but it's not working. What now?
   - Philippians 4:4,6,11
   - Ephesians 5:20
   - James 1:2-5

9

caring = encouraging one another

♥

My mom and I share one terrible habit. We both enjoy sporting events and are embarrassingly loud cheerers. This trait is perfectly acceptable at a Phillies or an Eagles game, but at Little League games it tends to be awkward.

I can remember my younger brothers saying, "Mom, please don't cheer for me, okay?" And I would sit at the other end of the stands with a friend so I wouldn't be stared at when people turned to look at the woman yelling speeches of encouragement to the whole team.

"Come on, Billy," Mom'd call to some little, mousy kid who was scared to death of the ball. "You can hit it a mile! I know you can!" And when Billy struck out, "Good try, Billy. Good try. That's the way to play the game!"

No wonder I told the kids they pasted their paper pumpkins well. It's genetic.

In high school I played basketball. I'm talking back in the era when women's rules limited us to half court and two bounces.

We played in the afternoon after school, and at the beginning of my first season Mom came to as many of our games as she could.

At first I was pleased at this evidence of her interest. No one else's mother came except the mom of the senior star of the team. The difference between this lady and Mom soon became apparent. While Mrs. Buck sat quietly in the nearly empty bleachers and smiled discreetly whenever her daughter scored, my mother cheered. Out loud. For everybody. Just like at Little League games.

When I suggested to Mom that perhaps she was too busy to keep the games on her schedule, I think she was relieved. She didn't have to worry about finding someone to watch my brothers or about finagling the car (in those days families had only one). I know I was relieved. The quiet of the gym, the main noise the squeak of sneakers on wood, was delightful.

Interestingly, when my kids played Little League, they asked of me the same thing my brothers and I had asked of my mother.

"Please don't cheer for me, Mom. Just watch."

In spite of Mom's predilection toward verbal encouragement, I loved it when she came to my school functions and my recitals and, eventually, college Parent's Days. And my kids loved it when I went to their things. Many is the wrestling or tennis match, soccer game or concert I have witnessed. To have someone there especially for you tells a child more than words ever could.

In fact, that's the basic definition of encouragement: *having someone there especially for you.* The dictionary says the meaning of encouragement is to give support to, to be favorable to. Vine's *Expository Dictionary of New Testament Words* offers "a calling to one's aid."[1] Crabb and Allender talk of "the kind of expression that helps someone want to be a better Christian, even when life is rough."[2] Paul spells it out to the Corinthians:

"I have great confidence in you; I take great pride in you. I am greatly encouraged; in all our troubles, my joy knows no bounds" (2 Corinthians 7:4).

Like I said, it's having your mom there yelling, "That's the way! Keep trying! I know you can do it!"

Encouragement is different from praise. Praise is ever given to God. We don't call encouragement to him because he doesn't need it. He isn't in process like we are. As the Great I Am, he needs no further development, no greater skills, no increased ability to cope. He is the Ultimate Finished Product, and we offer him praise for who he is and what he has done.

We, on the other hand, are rarely worthy of praise. Every so often we achieve enough to be applauded, to be complimented. But the greater need of our lives is encouragement because the greater experience of our lives is skinned knees, stubbed toes, and bruised hearts.

I've heard parents say that they don't want to compliment their kids because they don't want to give them a big head. Such a thought flies in the face of the life histories of all of us. Our kids face such criticism and so many closed doors in the mere act of being alive that we as parents need to encourage them all we can.

"Good try, Billy," we say when he strikes out, whether it's a ball-game, the classroom, the social scene, or the job market. "That's the way you play the game. I know you'll do better next time. Let God use this in your life to conform you to him."

And Billy will have the courage to try another time.

It's very easy to support a child when we are proud of him. He's just gotten all As. She's just been elected student body president. Moments like these are wonderful for any parent.

But most kids don't have these experiences. There's only one student body president each year and there may be several hundred seniors. How about the kids who don't make it to the top?

We parents weigh our children down with the burden of achievement expectations for several reasons, but a major one is that we parents want to be proud. We want to win the Mother of the Year Award. "Look at this fine kid," we want to say. "Isn't he/she great? He/she's MINE!"

When Chip was twelve, he came home from a Saturday afternoon with the guys feeling sick to his stomach. We sympathized and comforted him like the wonderful parents we envisioned ourselves to be.

"I even barfed at the field where we were playing football," he said, and we oohed and aahed all the harder.

"Did you catch a bug?" we asked. "Should we call the doctors? How about a spoonful of *Pepto Bismol?* Maybe you should go right to bed, even though it's only 5. A good night's sleep will help, you know."

I don't remember now what led Chip to confess, but he eventually admitted that he was sick to his stomach because he had been chewing a huge wad of tobacco, gotten tackled, and swallowed a bunch of it.

Suddenly his stomachache served him right, and we were no longer exemplary parents. After all, our dear son was chawin' tobacco with the boys! My Mother of the Year trophy was put on hold for another year.

All of our kids do dumb things, a good number do dangerous things, and many do illegal things in the process of growing up. By the grace of God, most survive.

Our job as Christian parents is to encourage them through the dumb, dangerous, and illegal things with the goal of a mature, contributing Christian adult always before us. God has forgiven us much; we need to forgive our kids.

"Come on, Billy. You can do it!"

"Come on, Chip. You don't want to chew tobacco. Not only is it hazardous to your health and a debatable Christian testimony, but it's also socially troublesome. What do you do with the saliva? Baseball coaches may let their players spit at the plate, but you'll find real people won't let you spit anywhere. You're a great kid. You don't want to chew tobacco. Besides, girls find it revolting."

It's vital our kids know we love them just as much during the bad times as the good. Obviously we're not as proud, but pride is when *we're* happy. Love and encouragement are for *their* happiness.

Complementary to encouraging one another is Paul's instruction, "Carry each other's burdens, and in this way you will fulfill the law of Christ" (Galatians 6:2).

Burdens are any things that press on us or make demands on our resources. Some burdens are emotional, some are physical. All are exhausting.

It's interesting that just two verses after Paul tells us to care for each other, he says that each of us should carry our own load. Is Paul contradicting himself? What does he want of us? Should we bear each other's burdens or bear our own?

Ideally we should all be able to care for ourselves, and most of the time most of us can. However all of us have times when we need someone desperately.

Maybe we've just lost our job.

Maybe we've become gravely ill and have four small children. Or maybe we just have four small children!

Maybe we're newly widowed, struggling to cope with the loneliness and fear of failure.

Maybe our teen-ager has become embroiled in a lifestyle that terrifies us.

Maybe the emotional pressures of living have become too much.

Certainly in all these situations and millions of others, the Lord is our ultimate Resource.

> God is our refuge and strength,
> an ever-present help in trouble. *Psalm 46:1*

However God is also the One who instructed us to be part of a body, and one purpose of this belonging is so that we will help each other.

> Let us not give up meeting together, as some are in the habit of doing, *but let us encourage one another—* and all the more as we see the Day approaching. *Hebrews 10:25, italics mine*

I readily admit I can become overwhelmed by the burdens I see that need bearing. And I readily admit that frequently I have no idea how to ease the burdens. I'm willing to help, but I don't know what to do.

Thankfully, the admonition of Scripture isn't to fix everyone's problems. It's to help them with the burden, to be there with encouragement.

Wayne and Vernann had been married only eight years when he died. She was devastated at the loss of the first person who had ever loved her unconditionally, the person whose love finally enabled her to believe in God's love. Shortly after Wayne's death, she wrote the following:

*People think pain is a hole, a void.
It's not.
It's an explosion, a giant coming apart from within.
But it doesn't end like a sudden violence.
It stays and stays and won't let go
Though you scream for it to stop.
I reach out for something, for anything.
Please make it stop. Please!*

*It doesn't stop; it doesn't let go.
It grabs my stomach;
It captures my thoughts.
I try to pretend it's not there,
But my words don't touch the thoughts
Trapped in the pain.*

*I wish for numbness,
Just not to think at all.
And sometimes I get it.
But the pain doesn't leave.
It just waits, to creep back in
And clutch me again and again.*

*Then God steps in.
"Oh, finally," I cry. "My pain will stop."
But it doesn't.
In fact, one by one, God removes everything
That held me together,
Even the picture of who I thought I was.*

*"God, how could you let this happen?
You have brought me to my knees.
You have left me nothing."*

*"Nothing but Me, dear child.
So take my hand; get off your knees.
We will walk together this time
And I will restore to you all that you need."*

*"But I can't believe You will.
How can I take Your hand and walk with You
When I can't believe?"*

*"You don't have to believe it, dear child.
You just have to do it."*

Every time I read these words, I am overwhelmed by the raw pain they illuminate. How can I ever help someone who is this anguished, who has hurt this deeply? I certainly can't say, "I understand." It would be a lie, one Vernann would recognize immediately.

Every morning I wave Chuck off to work, welcome him back each evening, sit across the table from him at dinner, climb into bed with him at night. I can't possibly comprehend agony like Vernann's with my husband safe by my side. Chances are someday I will, since most women become widows, but not now. And Vernann is in pain now.

Even if I don't comprehend the grief of a bereaved person, I can recognize things about the grieving process and at least intellectually understand them.

I can understand that there is a rootless feeling when you go to places you used to go as a couple, and for this reason church is one of the hardest places to go.

I can understand that just because people think it's time to get on with life doesn't mean the grieving person is ready to do so.

I can understand that it takes at least two years—twice through all holidays, birthdays, anniversaries—for things to seem "normal."

I can understand that there are times of overwhelming pain that preclude logical thought. The fact that these times will diminish through the months and years does not make this knowledge good comfort for the one in the middle of the grief. It sounds too much like the present pain is being minimized.

So we just say, "I love you. I'm so sorry. I wish I could make it easier for you. I promise to pray for you regularly."

"Be there," says Vernann. "You can't fix it. You can't make it better. You can't make it go away. But you can be there. Call. Visit. Write. Listen to the stories. Be there."

The grief group at church, of which Vernann is a member, jointly wrote the following:

> We are all around you. We are the ones who have lost husbands, wives, children, jobs, homes, health and/or families. We want you to know we are hurting.
>
> We don't expect you to understand because you haven't been there. We didn't understand either until it happened to us. We just wish we could convey the depths of our pain and how long it will last.
>
> We know that we will heal in God's time. We don't understand why, but God has ordained a grieving process that can take three years or more to grow through. The process is as individual as the person who is grieving and the personal situation.
>
> We have learned that grief cannot be hurried or set aside or gotten over or around. It must be worked through.
>
> We are each like a butterfly in a cocoon. It is hard work to emerge from that cocoon, but what a glorious result. And yet

if that cocoon is tampered with, or if you try to make the butterfly come out too soon, you will kill it.

It is like this with grief. Please don't try to force us from our cocoon until it is time. And please give us time to dry our wings in the SONshine until it is time for us to fly again.

We know God is with us and loves us. We know he is carrying us through the valleys and the peaks. We know there is a light at the end of the tunnel, but at the moment it seems so far away.

So be patient with us as we grow. Be patient with our tears, our anger, our forgetfulness, our out-of-character behavior, and especially our fragile feelings.

Thank you for the times you've prayed with us; for the times you let us cry without asking why; for the wordless hugs which told us you cared even when you didn't understand; for refraining from quoting Scripture as some kind of panacea.

Thank you for being there and know that we will be there for you when your time comes because we will understand your pain like no one else can.

It's vital to recognize that whether we're caring for someone like Vernann whose hurts are soul deep or someone like Chip whose stomachache was his own fault, we CANNOT meet all their needs. It's an absolute impossibility for any one person to care enough to defuse or heal the stresses of another. Just as no husband can be all a wife needs (or vice versa), no carer has the wisdom and strength for perfect encouraging and burden bearing.

But as Vernann says, we just have to be there.

Summary

Encouragement is having someone there especially for you. It differs from praise because it allows for people in process.

Parental pride is for the adult's happiness, but love and encouragement are for the child's.

Burden bearing is helping those whose circumstances make unusually heavy demands on their resources.

Even when we don't comprehend the emotion of a problem, we can still be there for the hurting person.

Questions, Questions . . .

1. When you recall your childhood, do you remember encouragement as part of it? Have you ever thanked your parents for their support? Or have you forgiven them for the hurt they inflicted? Why or why not?

2. If someone wanted to encourage you, what should they do for you? Would the same act encourage your husband/parent/child/friend?

3. When you see someone with deep pain like Vernann's, do you rush to help, or do you instinctively pull away? What does Acts 20:35 ask of us?

4. Read 2 Corinthians 1:3-5. What connection do these verses have with encouraging and burden bearing? What comfort can these verses give to one who has needed encouragement or help in bearing burdens?

10

caring = taking a chance

W E HAVE TWO CATS AT OUR HOUSE. WE THINK WE OWN THEM, but they know they own us.

One of the cats is big and gray and fluffy and is named, appropriately enough, Fluffy. He was given to Jeff several years ago to replace the kitten that had just passed on to his reward.

Fluffy is huge, weighing about twenty-two pounds. He loves to be held and purrs so loudly he keeps Chuck awake at night. When Jeff was younger, he used to carry Fluffy around his neck like an old lady would wear a fur tippet.

Our other cat, Bugs, is a beautiful white and gray monster with black lines like kohl around his eyes. I always think of Nefertiti when I look at him. We acquired him when he "followed" Chip home.

Rarely does Bugs want to be held. He likes to be near us, but not in our arms. If we do hold him, he seems to be in an emotional quandary, purring even as he angrily flicks his tail.

While both animals share the feline love of high places like tables, counters, and mantel pieces, other differences between the two are easily apparent.

Bugs guzzles food like a dog. Fluffy eats daintily and never gets to finish his bowl because Bugs shoulders him aside to devour whatever Fluffy hasn't yet ingested.

Bugs is a hunter, frequently bringing home treasures for our praise. In spite of being declawed, he catches squirrels, birds and rabbits, to say nothing of moles and mice. Fluffy catches June bugs.

The two personalities are fun to watch, and the cats get along very well in spite of their differences. They tussle regularly, leaping on each other, biting each other's rumps, punching each other in the head with their rear paws. And they groom each other, slurping and licking until one turns a lick into a nip and they're tussling again.

We Christians differ from each other just like the cats do. We belong to the same Lord, but here the similarities end. Nature and nurture have insured that we see the same issues through different eyes, and it is the multiple viewpoints that make caring such a challenge.

Some people want to be alone in their grief. Some people want company.

Some people are delighted when someone sends in one meal when they're ill. Some people expect food every night and are upset if they don't get it.

Some people are offended by a note saying, "I'm praying for you." To them it means someone thinks they aren't handling things well. Others are encouraged and uplifted by the same note.

Some people are embarrassed if friends come in to clean the house or mow the lawn in time of trouble. Others are grateful.

caring = taking a chance

These differences and the myriad others that make us each unique mean that our care will not always be received as we intend it. But that's all right. We know—and God knows—our motives.

There are three reasons why we can make ourselves vulnerable and willing to help in spite of people's differences and the unknown response we'll receive.

1. *God knows us and loves us whether or not people receive us and our help.*

One of the cornerstone truths of Scripture is that God loves us with a love that never changes. It doesn't increase because it's already perfect, and it doesn't decrease because God is constant.

> How great is the love the Father has lavished on us, that we should be called children of God! *1 John 3:1*

Imagine, if you can, the world and an orange side by side. The world will represent the love of God and the orange the love of people. The sheer magnitude of God's affection for us is beyond understanding. But if I am loved so thoroughly, I can risk.

One of my greatest spiritual insights in terms of impact in my daily living has to do with some small understanding of the God-love that envelops me. In his prayer in the Garden, Jesus says that God loves us as much as he loves his Son. "[You] . . . have loved them even as you have loved me" (John 17:23). God loves me—and you—as he loves Jesus! What a comforting, freeing, wonderful piece of truth!

I still want people to like me and appreciate what I do

because I'm human. But if they don't like me and what I do, it's okay because GOD LOVES ME AS HE LOVES JESUS!

2. The second reason I can be vulnerable and risk helping is that *everyone's got the same feelings deep inside.* Circumstances may differ, patterns of showing emotions may differ, but all humans are vulnerable. We all want to be loved. We all want to be appreciated. We all agonize when someone we love leaves our lives.

One of the things that makes adolescence so excruciating is that each kid thinks he or she is the only one who feels ugly or awkward or dumb. One of the things that should make adulthood more bearable is the realization that we all are vulnerable. No matter how suave and in control we look, we are all subject to anxieties and pressures. Paul calls us jars of clay to indicate how flawed we are (2 Corinthians 4:7).

Because you are as imperfect I am, I can risk serving you.

3. The third reason we can chance caring for one another is that *we want to be obedient children of our Father.* It is God's will that we help each other. There are over fifty verses in the New Testament that use the phrase "one another," each one with a command like "love" or "forgive" or "encourage" in it.

We often pray as the psalmist, "Teach me to do your will, for you are my God; may your good Spirit lead me on level ground" (Psalm 143:10).

In the "one another" verses we have part of the answer to this prayer. We have God's will revealed.

One day the mother of James and John asked a very impertinent and all-too-human favor of the Lord.

"Let my sons sit beside you in your kingdom," she said.

"You don't know what you're asking," Jesus told her. "Besides it's not my place to give out those seats. If you want to be first, you must be a servant, just as the Son of man did not come to be served but to serve and give his life a ransom for many" (Matthew 20:20-28, my paraphrase).

People's goals haven't changed much since Mrs. Zebedee spoke. Just watch a group of kids trying to line up. There's always a scramble to be first. Just watch a group of adults trying to keep up with the Joneses. Because of sinful hearts, a desire for position and happiness is still the chief motivation of many.

All of us who want to be carers in the pattern of Christ must accept that the goal of life is not position or happiness. It is conformity to Christ. It is becoming godly. It is to be givers, not receivers. It is to be servants.

Summary

We are all different and that makes caring difficult.
We can risk caring because:

- God loves us unconditionally.
- We are all flawed and in need.
- We want to obey God's will.

Happiness and position should not be our goals. Being conformed to Christ and becoming a servant should.

Questions, Questions...

1. Read 1 Corinthians 13:4-7. What do these verses have to say to those who care enough to get involved? *Love always protects, trusts, hopes, and perseveres. Love is kind.*

2. What happens when you try your best but you're not certain it's good enough? Read 1 Corinthians 15:58. *Stand firm and give yourself fully to the work of the Lord and know it is not in vain.*

3. Read 2 Corinthians 4:7. Why are we called jars of clay? What truth in this verse helps us when we get involved in caring? *When we serve we are of the Lord - the power is from the Lord not ourselves.*

4. Read 2 Corinthians 9:8. What is the comfort and encouragement offered here to those who care? *God is able to give you grace to be with you at all times.*

5. Read Galatians 1:10. What is the challenge to our motivation for service? *Are we trying to serve men or God?*

All acts have consequences.